PASSING THE TORCH

Luke O'Reilly

Passing the Torch

the columba press

First published in 1995 by
the columba press
93 The Rise, Mount Merrion, Blackrock, Co Dublin

Cover by Bill Bolger
Origination by The Columba Press
Printed in Ireland by Colour Books Ltd, Dublin

ISBN 1 85607 129 4

The author would like to thank Rosemary Fitzpatrick and Sandra Garry for typing the manuscript; Columbans, Pat Sales, Joe Flynn, Pat Sheehy, and Alo Connaughton for reading the drafts and for their very helpful comments; and Joe Flynn for proof-reading the final text.

By way of bibliography, I used the following books: *Early Church Portrait Gallery* (Maisie Ward); *My Country, My People* (Lin Yutang); *The Resurrection of the Chinese Church* (Tony Lambert); *The Church in China* (Fr Ladany SJ); *Communism and Man* (Frank Sheed); *Aristocracy of Soul* (Noel Dermot O'Donoghue); *St Patrick: His Life and Mission* (Helena Concannon); *St Patrick: Apostle of Ireland* (Fr Morris); *Dictionary of the Saints* (Donald Attwater); *What are Saints?* (Fr Martindale SJ); *One's Company* (Peter Fleming); *Growth in Holiness* (Fr Faber); *Spirituality of Founders* (Jim McCaslin); *The Beautiful and the Damned* (Scott Fitzgerald); *Golden Priest* (Aodh de Blacam); *The Best of Pearse* (Proinsias MacAonghusa and Liam Ó Riagáin).

Copyright © 1995, Luke O'Reilly

Contents

Foreword		7
	PROLOGUE: CELEBRATION	
1.	Arranging the St Patrick's Day Match	12
	PART I: MARTYRDOM IN SLOW MOTION	
2.	Martyrdom in Slow Motion	20
3.	Didn't Patrick have his Benignus?	27
4.	Our Benignus	32
5.	As Others See Us	44
6.	Faithful to Christ and to Rome	50
7.	A Picture to Remember	63
8.	A Saint of our own	69
9.	A Son among the Saints	76
10.	Soul Scan	84
11.	Columban Missionary	94
12.	Watchman for God in Nancheng	106
	PART II: THE WITNESS OF THE CHINESE PEOPLE	
13.	Pardon and Peace	118
14.	Prayer Power	126
15.	Our Morale Booster	131
	PART III: THE LEGACY OF BISHOP CLEARY	
16.	The Drama Producer	146
17.	The Teacher	162
18.	Back to our Roots	179
Epilogue		186

To Our Lady, Queen of the Missions,
and to our Columban co-missionaries, whether clergy or laity,
in Ireland, America, Australia, New Zealand,
Scotland, England, Wales,
this book is dedicated with gratitude and affection.

Foreword

My story is called *Passing the Torch*, and it deals with the ongoing Red persecution in the second half of this century in the Columban-staffed diocese of Nancheng, China. Four interweaving strands run through the narrative: the Red persecution; the Chinese Catholics who were called on to witness to their beliefs and to pass on the torch of the faith to their contemporaries, who might be wavering under the pressure, and to those who came after them. The third strand is the Columbans, especially the bishop, who had prepared both priests and people for the struggle ahead. And the fourth strand is the prayer power of our co-missionaries in the home countries.

My plan is to profile some Chinese Catholics and priests, who gave bold witness to their religion, and were a source of inspiration in varying degrees to their fellow Catholics. Many of the Nancheng Catholics are St Patrick's spiritual children because we baptised them and received them into the Church. I want to give them hope and to remind them that, as St Patrick shepherded us through the dark centuries of persecution, so he will also shepherd them and form them into a missionary race.

I also plan to profile at length a Columban, who died a year before I reached Nancheng. His name was Tom Ellis. The local Catholics regard him as a saint, and claim that they have obtained miraculous cures through his intercession. They went to his grave to pray even after the Communists forbade them, and they went to his grave even after we were expelled from China. The Nancheng Catholics would not want me to exclude him, because he is their saint. Besides, I am writing this story, primarily for them, because I want them to know about the proud

Christian heritage, which is theirs. I want them to realise how the generation before them witnessed to, and suffered for, their faith. But how did the Columbans get involved in China?

In 1916, a young secular priest from Cork, who had done four years missionary work in China, came home. He wanted to find a Maynooth professor, who would lead a national missionary movement to China. The priest's name was Edward Galvin. It happened that there was in Maynooth a young brilliant professor, who had already decided to go to China as a missionary. John Blowick was the professor's name. Providence brought the two priests together, and the Maynooth Mission to China, (as the Columbans were first known) was started.

When I profile Bishop Cleary, of Nancheng, he will tell you all about the origins of the Columbans, and about our co-founder, John Blowick. In Bishop Cleary, three strands of my story converge. The fine training he gave his Chinese priests prepared them for the ordeal of persecution. The efficient Catholic schools he built prepared the laity to resist the Communists. His intelligent and far-seeing leadership, for the three years before he was expelled, must have been a great help to his Chinese priests after his expulsion.

According to the story I heard, and I believe it was from Bishop Cleary I heard it, John Blowick had some difficulty in getting permission from his bishop to join the new missionary movement. When he wrote to Archbishop Healy of Tuam the archbishop said he could not afford to lose a priest of John Blowick's calibre, but that he wished the venture every blessing. John Blowick needed more than a blessing – even though it was the blessing of an archbishop; so he went to see the archbishop and he told him that 'a new era of missionary glory was at hand'. Whenever I read these words, I am always very amused, because only a very young priest could exude such confidence in the fall of 1916, when the mood of the country was one of dejection and World War I was still raging. John Blowick was only 28 years old. Archbishop Healy, his archbishop, on the other hand, was an old man, a scholar, an expert on Christianity in Ireland. But, against all human odds, the first band of Maynooth missionaries left for China on St Patrick's Day, 1920. I was only four and a half at the time, so I was unable to join them – unable to carry a torch – but I did go, however, with the band that left on the 22nd September 1946.

All of us old Nancheng hands will soon be dead and gone. All the valiant Chinese priests are already dead, except two, and they are too busy to write the record of Nancheng's continuing persecution. So I invite you to join us in spirit, so that you may be able to enter more deeply into the joys and sorrows, and glories of our persecution story. If it would be convenient for you to join us in spirit on St Patrick's Day 1948, that arrangement would suit us lovely.

PROLOGUE

Celebration

CHAPTER 1

Arranging the St Patrick's Day Match

Indeed we did celebrate St Patrick's Day in Nancheng. And how? Well, we wore the shamrock which had been mailed to us from the other end of planet earth. We did not 'drown it', because there was nothing available in which it could be decently drowned. Besides, we were nearly all Pioneers.

The highlight of the day was the Solemn High Mass at headquarters, usually celebrated by Bishop Cleary. The choir gave a very adequate and soulful rendering of the 'Mass of the Angels'. The choir was made up of seminarians, the Columban Sisters, catechists, a number of the laity, and as many of the priests round the diocese as could come in for the Feast. Incidentally, it was the bishop's feast day too. The plaintive soaring Kyries blended with the pointed and soaring Gothic arches of the Cathedral in a memorable and moving way, and I can still hear them across the decades 'like the memory of music on the breeze'.

After Mass, we mingled with and talked to the Chinese Catholics outside the Cathedral, and they invariably showed a great interest in the meaning of the shamrock. Then followed the next stage of the celebration – the match of the day no less – indeed the match of the year. Each St Patrick's Day, the Chinese priests, seminarians and catechists, played a team selected from the missionaries. Predictably the missionaries won, year after year.

We newly arrived missionaries objected to a state of affairs which made it virtually impossible for the Chinese to win a St Patrick's Day Match. Could we not have some arrangement whereby a few of the young missionaries would be 'transferred' to the Chinese Team, we asked? The older men said they preferred the traditional way, and that the Chinese most probably preferred it that way too. Fair enough. However, as it was only a friendly match, could we not let the Chinese win once, a win which no doubt would boost their confidence, and give them a keener interest in the game? They feared it would be difficult to do that without the Chinese losing 'face'. Without a doubt the 'face' factor had to be taken into account.

Still, beating the Chinese year after year, it seemed to me, looked like – yes – Irish Imperialism. But that could not be right because there were Columbans from Canada, the States, Scotland Australia, England, and they were all equally keen on winning the St Patrick's Day Match. Perhaps English-speaking Catholics feel they have something to prove on that day. So one just had to accept what one could not change.

Diocesan changes came about a year after our arrival in China and I was transferred from a city parish curacy, in the south of the diocese, to teach in the major seminary at headquarters. As well as running the diocese, the bishop taught in the seminary. I never dreamt that my appointment could, in any way, affect the outcome of the St Patrick's Day Match. Not till mid-February of the next year, 1948, when I got a letter from Peter Campbell and some of the other priests in the country asking me if I would select a missionary team, captain it, and make the necessary arrangements for the St Patrick's Day Match.

Overnight total power had been thrust on me – manager, skipper, selector all in one – and you know Lord Acton had something when he wrote 'Power tends to corrupt; absolute power corrupts absolutely', because my first decision was that the Chinese were going to win this one.

Vague plans were already forming in my mind as to how this might be achieved, without the missionaries suspecting that my commitment to their cause was less than total, or the Chinese suspecting that I was more than sympathetic to their aspirations. I needed badly to talk to somebody about the matter, but I could not very well talk to any of the football enthusiasts, as word might get out, and I would be sacked forthwith as manager, without even a 'rice handshake' never mind a 'golden one'.

So I toddled up to the bishop. We lived in the same house. I was in his room fairly often, because he was convinced St Paul wrote three letters to the Corinthians and that one of them has been lost, but that most of it was inserted here and there into the two letters we have. In his spare time he was trying to reconstruct the third letter – he would invite me to his room to check the Greek against his English translation.

I told him my hopes and half-formed plans. He had a deep, infectious laugh and he just roared. 'Of course,' he said, 'I'd love to see the Chinese win, but I can't see it happening with all these big fellows out to clobber them.'

Encouraged by the enlightened episcopal outlook, I proceeded with my strategy and tactics. My strategy was taken from golf. I would 'handicap' the missionaries, just as a good golfer is penalised by having strokes taken from him, so that the mediocre golfers against whom he is playing in a competition may have a chance.

Fair enough. I penalised the missionaries by giving them a weak last line of defence. The rector of the seminary I selected as right-back. He was an American, Pat Gately. He had played American football – and this would be no asset to him in playing soccer. He was, as a Chinese who spoke broken English said about another man, 'plenty too fat' as well. For goalkeeper, I selected Peter X, who was nearly fifty, and his sight was not perfect. I did not know then that he was colour blind! This only came to light when he picked up a red biretta – a Monsignor's – thinking it was a black one, and wore it on his way to the altar in a big American Church the following year. I selected myself for the left-back because I felt this was the position in which my sympathy for the legitimate aspirations of the Chinese team could find its most practical and effective expression.

So confident were the missionary team that this weak last line of defence caused not the slightest raising of a missionary eyebrow, never mind criticism. The possibility of being beaten was just unthinkable. Peter X had played in goal in the past.

We had a handwritten Gaelic football manual in St Jarlath's, the boarding school to which I went. We called it the 'Koran'. Today, some may think that our choice of the name showed a remarkable ecumenical outreach in young boys in the early '30s and that we were well ahead of our time in this field. Be that as it may, according to the sound football doctrine of the 'Koran', a player must beat his opponent to the ball every time, and a defender must practically never kick the ball across his own goal. My tactics were to go contrary to the sound teaching of the 'Koran'. So, in briefing Pat Gately, I told him not to worry if the young speedy seminarians beat him to the ball and that, if he found himself cornered when defending, he could kick the ball across our goal in the hope that another missionary might get it.

As captain, much was expected of me. So in the early stages, I had to give some sign of commitment and hunger for the ball etc. I dashed down the wing, beating my opponent to the ball and made a good clearance or, alternatively, slung the ball across to a loose striker. Other times, I fell just before reaching the ball or cleared it across the goal. With a little practice, one can 'slice' a ball to the right, while giving the impression one is kicking it down the wing. Such tactics, coupled with Pat Gately's lack of speed, were partly responsible for the two goals slammed home by the seminarians. Though the missionaries had three good strikers, they only managed one goal in the first half.

This was largely due to the outstanding performance of the tall Chinese goalie. He was a catechist, a most zealous one, and had instructed many groups in the city and many villagers in the countryside. He had a very nice tenor voice and became known as 'John McCormack'.

'McCormack' was even better in the second half and his display put heart and determination into his team-mates. In spite of the almost unrelenting pressure to which he was subjected, he conceded nothing for the first thirty-five minutes. Then he was beaten by a rasper of a shot which nobody could have saved. But the Chinese kept coming back, galvanised by 'McCormack's' inspiring performance.

At five minutes to go and the score level, they were attacking down the left wing where I was defending. To relieve the pressure, I sliced the ball to the right and across our goal. From nowhere came Peter Hsiu, the best of the seminarians, got possession and dribbled the ball towards our goal. Peter X ran out to intercept him but, with a neat swerve, he side-stepped and before you could say 'The Leith police dismisseth us', Peter had slammed home his team's third goal. The Chinese were jubilant. The missionaries were frustrated. And then I saw a sight unparalleled in the annals of football – two missionaries galloping in the direction of the manager/captain from the other end of the field. When they reached me, they were panting like two greyhounds who had just finished a 525 yard race. The first of them, Hugh Bennett, a native of Liverpool, who had played second division with West Bromwich Albion before becoming a Columban missionary, upbraided me: 'What do you jolly well mean, Luke?' Peter Campbell, a brilliant Tyrone and Ulster Gaelic footballer was the second man. He just said, sternly, 'Play up, mon.'

I thought the 'stiff upper lip' was the only fitting response to such an outrage. The game is devalued when this kind of conduct from players is tolerated. As manager, I could have disciplined them, but it was not that easy. Remember, we were 'east of Suez' and, besides, they were always close friends.

In the last moments of the game, the missionaries mounted a 'do or die' attack, but 'McCormack' remained unshaken, and unshakeable. And, when the final whistle went, the Chinese were winners by 3:2 for the first time ever. They went wild with joy, and the people ran on to the pitch to congratulate them. 'McCormack' was the hero of his team. I felt like the 'bad guy' in a Western, as unadmiring looks were thrown at me by some of the missionaries.

At tiffin, (lunch) wise-cracks were made about my competence as a manager. Frantic efforts at being funny about my judgement as selector were being made by serious-minded men. The presence of four or five Chinese priests cramped the style of our humourists quite a bit. When I was under siege, so to speak, an episcopal mini-wink from the top of the table brought relief.

THE ST PATRICK'S DAY MATCH

After siesta, we went over to the Columban Sisters' convent for tea, a sing-song and Benediction. At night, there was a game of bridge or poker in the bishop's house. That was the last St Patrick's Day Match, on March 17, 1948.

When the feast came round again, the Red Army was poised north of the Yangtze River ready to cross, and to strike at the heartland of Central South China. We moved the seminarians to another seminary in a far distant place. I was sent as pastor to a parish away up in the hills where the tigers used to come down and eat the pigs.

PART I

Martyrdom in slow motion

CHAPTER 2

Martyrdom in slow motion

By St Patrick's Day, 1950, the Reds had taken over the whole country. Mao Tse Tung had declared that the defeated Nationalists were traitors and must be eliminated. In their Constitution, the Reds declared that there was freedom of religion. That was their official policy but an unofficial persecution was taking place in our diocese anyhow, since shortly after their arrival. On St Patrick's Day, 1952, there were only three Columbans left in the diocese of Nancheng and by St Patrick's Day, 1953, all the Columbans had been driven from the diocese and nearly all the foreign priests had been driven from China.

I have described how valiantly the Chinese team struggled for victory on that last St Patrick's Day Match in 1948. From 1950 onwards, they became engaged in a more deadly struggle. It was a struggle against 'angels of darkness' unleashed during the Red persecution. Now, in 1993, forty-five years later, I would like to show you highlights from both struggles on the film of memory: the struggle against the 'angels of darkness' and the struggle against the Columbans.

'*John McCormack*'
As your commentator, my first duty is to nominate 'John McCormack', the Chinese goalkeeper as the 'man of the match'. We priests never called him anything except 'McCormack', though I did know that his Chinese name was Hse – but that is another story and I will return to it shortly. For the moment, look how he dives to the right and to the left to stop the piledrivers from Peter Campbell and Malachy Toner, who were in their early thirties and who were very effective strikers. But 'McCormack' turned in a four-star performance that day.

At this stage the picture of McCormack the footballer gets a bit faded, so I shall show you a picture of McCormack, the four star catechist, in action. Look at him going out, day after day, to bring the good news to many villages in the Nancheng area. He is going out to villages where the people had showed an interest in Christianity. Look at him going out most nights to instruct groups of people who wanted to become catechumens. Notice how he continues his apostolic activities for a year and a half after the Reds took over. His wife did complain to Barney O'Neill that her husband was so busy at this work that he was away from home all day, till late at night. Observe him come to visit me the day after I had been expelled from my parish and escorted to Nancheng to await my trial at a higher tribunal. He was very anxious to hear about my experiences as I was the first priest in the diocese to be brought before the People's Court and expelled from my parish. I can see him now as he listens carefully to what I have to say. Notice he is a tall man for a southern Chinese, slim, with short cropped hair and in his mid thirties.

Some of the priests, and indeed the bishop, had thought I would get back to the parish again after land division was finished. McCormack did not share their hopes. See how he talks to me slowly and with great conviction. My expulsion, he tells me, is the beginning of a large scale persecution in the diocese and in the country. The Reds have warned him that he is the 'marked man' amongst the Catholics of the diocese. His fate, as he saw it, on that dark December evening in 1950, was pain, torture, death for his faith. Observe, he begins to speak more rapidly as he gives me a frightening demonstration of the tortures that await him. All I can remember, at this distance of time, about that demonstration is that he held the index finger of his left hand between the thumb and index finger of his right, I took this to indicate how they might pull off his finger nails, or perhaps break some of his fingers in jail. Still, that December evening, he was at peace, because he believed he was called to witness to Christ by his sufferings and death. He felt privileged. He talked like a man whose acts of acceptance and renunciation had already been made. When I think of him, now, a poem by Pádraic Pearse comes to mind. 'Renunciation' is the title of the English translation. The lines I think of are:

> I have turned my face to this road before me,
> to the deed that I see, and the death that I shall die.

To me, these lines express the renunciation and resolution of McCormack as we talked together.

McCormack's reading of the situation proved accurate. Within a year, all the Columbans, except Bishop Cleary, Seamus O'Reilly and I, had been forced out of the country. On 8 February 1952, two Chinese priests, Jim Yang, John Chang and we Columbans, were publicly tried as criminals in Nancheng. I should have said that one layman was tried with us. Guess who it was? McCormack, of course. From the day over a year earlier that the Communists told him he was a 'marked man', he had worked his way swiftly up the Red crime charts. On that February day he found himself on equal footing with a criminal like myself who was charged with multiple sabotage.

Like all Chinese, he was 'face' conscious. Marched through the streets of his native city, beaten, kicked and spat upon in the company of us foreign criminals, was for him the depth of degradation. Watched by his friends and neighbours, wife and relatives and family – all that filled his cup of sorrow to the brim. I wonder did he catch a glimpse of his wife as he went on his *Via Dolorosa* that afternoon? Steeling himself to the fact that he was leaving his wife and family forever must have been his most bitter agony. According to seminarian Tommy Yu, McCormack's family consisted of two girls. They were only school children. Still they brought him food, when allowed to visit the jail.

Had he joined the Patriotic Church and rejected the Pope, he would have been given a top post. Indeed, I am certain that the Nancheng leaders of the Patriotic Church did their best to enlist McCormack as a member. They would have pointed out to him that bishops and priests up and down China had already joined under pressure, and in doing so had shown themselves to be patriotic Chinese Catholics. Some of them would even have said that in their hearts they still acknowledged the Pope as head of the Church. They would have assured him that their lip service and their signatures was all they gave to the Patriotic Church. I can see McCormack quoting for them the pertinent texts from scripture, and warning them that we must confess our Lord before all people, not only with our hearts but with our lips. McCormack also knew his history. He would have reminded the educated leaders of the Patriotic Church in Nancheng of the lessons to be learned from the English Reformation. Henry VIII demanded that he be recognised as head of the Church in England and that the Pope should be rejected. Some bishops and priests under pressure, or through fear, gave him that recognition. St John Fisher and that merry martyr, St Thomas More, amongst others, remained faithful to the Pope and were put to death by Henry VIII. He hoped, with God's help, to follow the footsteps of these two great saints and martyrs.

After our trial on 8 February 1952, the two Chinese priests and McCormack were jailed. Jim Yang and John Chang had cells near each other and were able to communicate from time to time. McCormack was in some other part of the jail and for a time we heard nothing about him. Then we heard that he was doing hard labour. Later a Chinese told us that he was in chains. Later still, we learned that he was being tortured. Bishop Cleary, Seamus O'Reilly and I were forced out of China less than a year after the priests and McCormack were imprisoned. After that, we had little news from Nancheng until we got a letter, thirty years later, from Jim Yang.

It was a very comprehensive report of the heroism of our Chinese priests and of many of the ordinary Catholics. We received it in 1980 and Bishop Cleary had been dead ten years at that time. But for me, the letter left one big question mark. Why was there no mention of McCormack? What happened to him? As a result, I concluded that McCormack had died so early on in the persecution that Jim, writing in 1980, would have forgotten about it. Jim Yang did speak in his letter about a heroic catechist called Matthias Hsu, but I took it for granted that Matthias was a catechist, whom we called Matt, from a place called Pakan, twenty miles from Nancheng. I have to humbly confess now that I have been reading that letter time and time again, since 1980 and it is only in November 1993 that it struck me that Matthias Hsu could be McCormack. I wrote to Seamus O'Reilly in the States to ask his opinion because he knew McCormack better than I did. He said that he always understood that Matthias Hsu was McCormack. Hse or Hseh could be the local dialect and Hsu would be the Mandarin, in his opinion. It was only when I heard Pat Sheehy, another Nancheng priest, corroborate Seamus' opinion, that the depth of my dim-wittedness came home to me. Matt Yu was the catechist I had in mind.

Here is the relevant paragraph from Jim Yang's letter:

> When I was in Nancheng prison (1959), I met our heroic catechist Mathias Hsu, who was for weeks locked up next to my cell. We were all starved so badly that we could hardly walk without holding on to one thing or another. We could not see each other, but we encouraged each other by singing the holy songs. The poor fellow got very ill in jail and he was sent home for medical treatment. He died some time in 1959. He gave an excellent example to the Catholics, in spite of the fact that he was in dire straits, as his wife had left him to live with another man, and that he had to cut firewood to earn his living. He was still optimistic and loyal to the Church to the end of his life. It is no wonder the good Catholics and pagans who knew him would give him a tiptop appraisal whenever he is talked about.

McCormack was easily the strongest man on that team in 1948 and yet he was the first to die. Jim Yang met him in October 1959 and he died within that year, about seven years after he was imprisoned. He was beside Jim, so it would appear that he was not sent home for medical treatment till well into November. We do not know what type of medical treatment he received. We do know that a man who was unable to walk without holding on to something, as a result of starvation, and who got very ill according to Jim, had to cut firewood to earn his living. The winter can be bitterly cold in Nancheng. A criminal like McCormack would be kept under surveillance after his release. Some neighbours might be afraid to help him, because to do so would be regarded as a crime by the authorities. As far as we know, he died in pain, from torture and chains. Though rejected by his wife, he had the consolation of having his daughters with him at the end.

The hope that he would win the martyr's crown in the traditional sense, like St John Fisher and St Thomas More who shed their blood for Christ, was unfulfilled. But perhaps, as a result of the Communist persecution, we should rethink the whole theology of martyrdom. The reason is this: the Communists did not want to make Catholic martyrs after the 1940s. They claimed to have had their own martyrs and they appreciated the impetus a martyr can give to a cause for which he or she is prepared to die. The treatment McCormack received during his seven-years in jail was a kind of martyrdom in slow motion. It took him to the gates of death and left him there.

Jim Yang's last sentence is a thought-provoking one. 'It is no wonder the good Catholics and pagans who knew him would give him a tiptop appraisal'. A 'tiptop appraisal' would mean that the people of Nancheng saw McCormack as a man who witnessed to his faith and to his Lord by his sufferings and death during the persecution. Persecution seems to ferry us across the centuries to the early church, to the age of the martyrs. In the first two centuries of Christianity, there were eleven persecutions. There was an enthusiasm, which we in the twentieth century find hard to understand, to win the martyr's crown. There was a desire to share in Christ's passion and thus further his redemptive work. Martyrdom, they believed, was a kind of missionary effort which brought converts from paganism into the Church. A well known Christian writer named Tertullian has written, 'the blood of martyrs is the seed of Christians'.

This desire to respond to Christ's love, and thereby spread his good news, became almost a contagion in the age of the martyrs. Maisie Ward in her book, *Early Church Portrait Gallery*, tells the story of Origen, a famous figure in the early church. He was born in 180 AD in Alexandria, Egypt. Origen's father died in the persecution of 202 AD. His mother had to hide Origen's clothes to prevent him from going to martyrdom with his father. She did this because she had younger children and Origen was the sole support of the family after his father's death. Origen became a great teacher in the Church of that period, even though he did make mistakes in his teaching later. Though he became very famous, he never forgot that he was a son of a martyr and never ceased to hope that one day he himself would die for Christ. Like McCormack, his hope was unfulfilled.

That picture of McCormack on that December evening 1950, when he came to talk to me, fascinates me. There he stands fit and full of health, hoping and wishing that he would be given the privilege of shedding his blood for Christ. His wish was not granted in the way he had hoped. His life was an inspiration to those of us who knew him during the persecution.

There is some consolation for us twentieth-century people in the words of an early Irish monk who wrote: 'There is red martyrdom and white martyrdom. Red martyrdom is achieved when one gives up his life for a sacred cause. White martyrdom is the daily dying to oneself.' Another early Irish monk, St Columban, in his motto tells us how this dying to self may be achieved: 'Let us be Christ-centred, not self-centred'. To become Christ-centred we have to die daily to the different manifestations of self, self-centredness, self-importance, self-indulgence, self-promotion, self-pity, inordinate self-love. So we Christians of this century have an opportunity of doing quite a lot of dying, and doing that day after day is 'white martyrdom'.

Of course, there is pain in white martyrdom, but not as much, I venture to think, as in the martyrdom in slow motion which McCormack suffered. If ever a man followed Our Lord's injunction and laid up for himself treasure in heaven, that was McCormack.

CHAPTER 3

Didn't Patrick have his Benignus?

The next figure I want to focus on is Fr Jim Yang, who was captain of the Chinese team in that St Patrick's Day Match, 1948, to the best of my recollection. Jim was a convert to Catholicism. He and his parents and his brother, Philip, were received into the Church in Nanfeng, about thirty miles from Nancheng, when Jim was twelve years old. At the ripe old age of eleven, he already had a broken engagement behind him. But we should not conclude from this that he was a youngster in a hurry. In the affairs of the heart, in that part of China, the matchmaker played a major role. Through the services of the matchmaker, children could get engaged from eight years onwards. Jim's father would have gone to the matchmaker and asked him to find a suitable bride for his eight-year-old son. The matchmaker then would go through his waiting list of potential brides. Then he would go into what we call nowadays, a period of discernment, to figure out which of them would be the most suitable. Then he would report back to Jim's father. If Jim's father were pleased with what he heard, he would ask the matchmaker to enquire about the girl's name and the moment of her birth. He would do this, so that the horoscopes of the boy and girl might be examined in order to ascertain if the proposed marriage would be a happy one. Sometimes an astrologer would be called in to compare the horoscopes; sometimes the matchmaker was an astrologer. If the horoscope proved positive, then the betrothal followed.

It was binding on both parties, although there were five other ceremonies before the wedding day, which might not take place for many years. In the Chinese customs surrounding marriage, there was little place for love at first sight. The first sight the boy got of the girl was the day of the wedding, when the veil would be lifted from her face. The boy was often disenchanted with what he saw. He realised with a pang that the beauty and poise and graciousness of the bride-to-be, as described by the matchmaker, existed only in the eye of the beholder – the matchmaker. Thus it was that matchmakers had a very bad press in parts of China. The phrase 'to lie like a matchmaker' came into common usage.

How Jim managed to disengage from the betrothal I cannot remember. I should know because Pat Dermody, who was pastor in Nanfeng at the time, told me. Perhaps the professional services of the matchmaker were again required so that no 'face' might be lost by the girl or her family. Perhaps becoming a Catholic and planning to become a priest would be a sufficient reason in the eyes of all concerned. After his decision to become a priest, Jim went to Nancheng school to finish his studies, and then entered the major seminary, where he was ordained on 20 December 1942. Bishop Cleary supervised his education and taught him a number of subjects. After ordination, the bishop sent Jim to the University of Amoy in the province of Fukien, to study Chinese Civil Law. He must have been two or three years there, because when we arrived in China in the beginning of December 1946, he was back teaching in the seminary, and he had obtained his degree in Chinese Civil Law.

In 1947 I was appointed to the major seminary and got to know Jim quite well during the year that I was there. We became good friends. He had beautiful manners, as you would expect from an educated Chinese, and he had a lot of consideration for other people and a lot of kindness. The Chinese are supposed to be a phlegmatic race but there was a certain fire in Jim's make-up too. He would share with us some witty sayings from the Chinese sages during conversation. He was the first Chinese priest who got all his training from the Columbans and he had a very good influence on all the Chinese seminarians. He could be quite entertaining.

One incident from days in the Nancheng seminary with Jim Yang stands out. The early summer months of 1948 were oppressively hot; even the Chinese noticed this. In the seminary we just wore T-shirts or sweatshirts. We sweated so much that we had to change our sweatshirts two or three times a day. The result of this was that I might have four or five sweatshirts on the line each day, and that the laundry was kept extremely busy. But when some of the Chinese saw Jim Yang having an equal number of sweatshirts on the line too, they expressed their disapproval. They felt that a Chinese should not have as many sweatshirts as a foreigner. A few of the foreign priests joined in the chorus of disapproval, saying that it would spoil Jim Yang and that it was not the proper training for a Chinese priest. In the 40s, I suppose we regarded ourselves as superior to the Chinese. As students, we had laughed at Kipling's attitude towards the Orient, and I quote:

> Ship me somewhere east of Suez
> where the best is like the worst.
> Where there aren't no ten commandments
> and a man can raise a thirst.

Still we had caught something of that colonial mentality. Kipling had also spoken of 'lesser breeds within the law'. That kind of attitude can be contagious in the Orient, and the missionary must be careful not to catch it.

However, when some of the priests told Bishop Cleary that they felt Jim Yang was being spoiled, he said that his policy was to treat the Chinese priests exactly as he treated foreign priests. The bishop put a lot of time and work into Jim's formation. I expect he hoped that Jim would be a model for future priests to be trained by the Columbans. I thinks he was training Jim for leadership, maybe hoping that he would be a successor of his, and be capable of leading the Catholic community through any kind of ordeal. Again, some of the priests thought that the bishop was giving too much time to Jim and they told him so. He was that kind of man; you could say what you liked to him, and he would weigh up impartially the value of what you said, and he would always be gentle in that type of situation. This time his reply to the priests concerned was a gentle question. The question was 'Did not Patrick have his Benignus?' The reply was terse, unexpected and dramatic.

When we young missionaries arrived in China in 1946, some of the older priests related the incident to us, and they regarded it as a very funny story. It is the decent thing to laugh at a story when the story teller thinks it is funny, although it may not always be the honest thing. Few of us are as honest as was my friend and neighbouring pastor in China, Mike Halford, when I told him a funny story which I promised would make him 'die laughing'. His honest verdict was 'that story is more to be pitied than laughed at', and I can assure you I laughed long and loud at his verdict, without the slightest bit of self pity. One day Mike and a young school boy came into the house in Nancheng. Mike had a hold of the young boy's hand. Another priest remarked 'I see you have a young disciple Mike?' 'Didn't Patrick have his Benignus?' retorted Mike.

When I look back now in 1995 and think of Bishop Cleary's dramatic, gentle, brief reply to the priests who criticised him, I feel his words were tinged with prophecy. I think this because the part played by Jim Yang in Patrick Cleary's apostolate were very like the part played by St Benignus in St Patrick's apostolate. As well as that, the relationship between Patrick Cleary and Jim Yang was very similar to the relationship between St Patrick and St Benignus.

In her book, *St Patrick: His Life and Mission,* Helena Concannon tells us that God gave Patrick Benignus amongst the first fruits of his apostolate (if not the very first). It appears that Patrick ordained a native boy or two, who had been trained by pre-Patrician priests. Benignus would seem to have been the first boy whom Patrick received into the Church and trained and ordained. Furthermore, Benignus was the beloved disciple of St Patrick. Patrick Cleary ordained John Chang who had got most of his training from the French Vincentians, but as I have noted, Jim Yang was the first priest to be received into the Church, trained and ordained by Patrick Cleary and the Columbans. Jim, too, was the beloved disciple.

During his first Lent in Ireland, in 433, St Patrick met Benignus. Seschen, a Chieftain, from Gormanstown area of County Meath, had Patrick as his guest and the boy developed a great affection for the saint. When the saint was leaving, Benignus begged his father and cried piteously as he did so, to allow him to become a follower of the saint. The father had no choice except to give his permission. Benignus was only a teenager, I suppose, when he became a member of St Patrick's retinue.

Benignus played a part in all the great events that render memorable St Patrick's first Easter in Ireland. He helped to kindle the paschal fire on Slane on Easter Saturday night, 26 March, 433. When Patrick and his followers were summoned to the King's presence in Tara, one of the King's magicians challenged Patrick to an ordeal by fire. Remarkably enough, Patrick chose Benignus to be his representative in this strange combat of fire. Through Patrick's prayer, Benignus won the combat and came through the ordeal of fire unscathed, whereas the magician was burned alive.

CHAPTER 4

Our Benignus

Jim Yang, Patrick Cleary's Benignus, was our representative in very many ordeals, from the arrival of the Communists in May 1949, to February 1952, when Jim was put in jail. In these tension-laden years, it was Jim who went to the County Commissar to defend us, when we country priests were declared criminals one by one. The County Commissar and his staff respected Jim not only for his knowledge of their country's laws, but also for the fact that he was a very educated man.

But if the fact that Jim was highly educated won respect from the Communists, the fact that he was always pleading for foreigners incurred their hatred. Some of them said to him 'Are you Chinese?' Such a question is regarded by the Chinese as very offensive and insulting. His most difficult ordeal during that period was when he had to repeat Bishop Cleary's excommunication of the leaders of the Patriotic Church. The County Commissar warned him that he would suffer for his words from the pulpit, and that the Chinese would spit on his grave.

However, his real ordeals started when he was imprisoned in Nancheng on the 8 February 1952, although he was set free on a number of occasions for short periods. During his years in jail, he suffered the ordeals of brainwashing and torture (hard and soft tactics). He suffered the ordeal of starvation as I have noted in my account of John McCormack's sufferings in jail. Another painful ordeal he suffered was the whippings he received in prison while being suspended in mid air. We do not have any indication of how often he went through the ordeal of whippings, but I should think the Communists whipped him until they realised there was no hope of getting him to join the Patriotic Church.

But there were other ordeals. Shortly before Easter 1957, the Archbishop of Nanchang, Archbishop Chou, was released from jail. Our Nancheng priests were also enjoying what Jim calls 'semi freedom'. But, best of all, the seminarians, who had gone to Shanghai seminary to finish their studies as we were leaving China in January 1953, returned to Nancheng. Jim decided to invite Archbishop Chou to come to Nancheng and ordain them. At first, the government gave permission but then the Provincial Bureau of Religious Affairs in Nanchang rescinded the permission given by the local authorities in Nancheng. They said that due to the poor health and old age of the archbishop, they could not allow him to go to Nancheng. Jim comments in his letter: 'How thoughtful they were, and how considerate they were. Shameful hypocrites. The real reason why they were ready to eat their words was that they wanted to spoil the soup with a dead rat.' The upshot was that Jim and Paul Yu took the three seminarians to Nanchang and asked the archbishop to ordain them there. He agreed, but then the trouble started.

Now in Nanchang, there were two Chinese priests who had made false charges against Archbishop Chou; they had told the Communists, after their arrival, that he had collaborated with the Japanese when he was a bishop in the north of China. They were automatically excommunicated, because of the false charges they had made. When they heard that the archbishop was to ordain three Nancheng seminarians, one of them, the leader called Hu, insisted on taking part in the ceremony as deacon or sub-deacon, I suppose. Jim told them that this was against Canon Law, and one of the apostate priests threatened to beat him up and lock him in a room. The archbishop looked up the books on theology and Canon Law and decided that as he was the ordaining prelate he could dispense with the assistance of other priests and so the problem was solved fairly peacefully and three very fine seminarians became priests of Nancheng diocese.

They returned to Nancheng and the people were delighted that they had three young priests of their own. Catholics from Pakan, Kiutu, Chuliang, came in to Nancheng for Easter Sunday, and there were seven priests present at the solemnity. But Jim tells us that even during the Easter Season he was already preparing for another combat, a more subtle and potentially dangerous type of ordeal. The Reds hoped that, although whippings and torture and brain washing failed to persuade Jim to join the Patriotic Church, that sweet reasonableness might achieve this result.

With this in mind, they told Jim that many a bishop and archbishop, much more learned than he was in Theology and Canon Law, had, in fact, joined the Patriotic Church. They said that these bishops and archbishops were always of higher ecclesiastical rank than he was. 'Did my stubbornness not show that I was looking for trouble when I rejected what prelates of higher rank in the Church accepted? they asked.' I replied that as a Roman Catholic, I looked on the Pope as the Vicar of Christ and I would remain loyal to the Pope, even if it cost me my life. I told them too, although they didn't like the word, that they were persecuting the Church. I assured them of the fact that the blood of martyrs would always be the seed of Christianity as it had been in Tertullian's time during the persecutions in the third century. On hearing this, Jim continues in his letter, 'they of course laughed at me'.

A few months later, they changed their strategy. They asked Jim to go to see the other places and to see what the bishops and archbishops had done and were doing in the Patriotic Church and to consult with them on the matter. When Jim refused to fall in with their new strategy, they asked him to write letters to various bishops and archbishops discussing the question of joining the Patriotic Movement with them, and requesting them to point out the principles on which they justified themselves. At first, Jim refused to write the letters, which they suggested. Let me again quote from Jim's letter:

> But, having pondered deeply over the matter, I came to the conclusion that it might be a good opportunity to encourage some of those old prelates by informing them that in one of the smallest dioceses in China there were still eight native priests standing firmly against the attack launched by our enemy on our religious belief. I would be proud too to let them know that, despite the fact that our whole community

consisted of only eight priests, none of us were going to be a shameful turncoat. Indeed, every one of us always reminded ourselves that, being the fruits of Bishop Cleary's apostolic work in Nancheng, we should not be unworthy children of St Columban, neither should we be unfaithful clients of our Blessed Lady, the Queen of the Holy Rosary. For this reason, I finally agreed to write a circular letter to the bishops or the vicars of those places, on condition that I should be free to express my own opinion on the matter for the exchange of outlook. They consented to this. Then I sent out a circular to about fifty different places according to the addresses they gave me. I remember I sent one to the Archbishop of Xenjang, one to the Bishop of Szechuan (who was actually consecrated by Pope Pius XI), another to Shanghai and yet another to Nanking etc.

Some of them in their replies said that the matter was too delicate to be talked about in a letter. They asked me to go to their places and discuss the matter with them personally. The only thing was, according to them, that everyone should act in accordance with his own conscience. How timid they showed! They were all afraid to face the problem in a manly way. Most of them got my letter but kept silent. Of course, I did put them into a puzzling dilemma from which they could not escape merely by saying 'yes' or 'no' because I put before them a lot of questions on Theology and Canon Law. I requested them to answer the questions and explain the quotations in Canon Law which I mentioned in the letter.

It was up to them, I said, to plead the reasons for their behaviour and their attitude towards the movement and towards the Church situation in China. Though I did not get any satisfactory reply from any of them, some good results were brought about. *Deo gratias*. As one of the cadres in the police office in Nancheng told me in 1959, two years after I had been arrested again, the letters I sent out to the bishops and the vicars were utterly reactionary, and caused a terrible confusion among the prelates. So much so, as I was informed afterwards, that some who had joined the Patriotic Church actually turned over on receiving my letter. Naturally, I was blamed for having dispatched such a circular letter; it was even one of the accusations they brought against me.

When Jim says that some of the prelates turned over on receiving his letter, he means, I would say, that they left the Patriotic Church and renewed their loyalty to the Pope. He does not say how many, I suppose he did not know himself. Every page of the twenty-four page letter Jim sent to us in 1980 was joyful news. But the courage and competence with which he dealt with the ordeal of being caught between the heads of the Bureau of Religious Affairs in Jiangxi province and the bishops and archbishops who had joined the Patriotic Church, that news was more than joyful – it was a glorious surprise. They hoped that Jim would be brought into the Patriotic Church by those learned archbishops and bishops. Jim turned the tables on them, by bringing some of these prelates back to full union with the Roman Catholic Church.

When I look back at the terror and the tension under which the people lived in Communist China, I just marvel at what Jim did. In our wildest imaginings, we priests who were in Nancheng with Jim could never dream that he would be capable of such leadership. All we hoped for was that he and our other priests would keep the faith, lie low, not look for trouble and help Catholics whenever they got the opportunity.

In fact, during the years since we left China, before we got Jim's letter, we were worried. We had been hearing that very many Chinese priests had, under pressure, joined the Patriotic Church, and we feared that some of our priests would have succumbed to the wiles and the threats of the Communists. Maybe at the back of our minds, too, there was a little of that Western superiority which would say that the Chinese are not able to take it. I was placing limits to the power of the Holy Spirit. Words from St Paul's letter to the Ephesians, Chapter 3, verse 20, rebuked me the first time I read them after getting Jim's letter. The words are: 'Glory be to him whose power, working in us, can do infinitely more than we can ask or imagine, glory be to him from generation to generation in the Church, and in Christ Jesus forever and ever, Amen.'

In his letter to us, Jim Yang wrote: 'What a great pity that our Bishop Cleary to whom I owe so much has left us.' And how happy and proud he would have been that his 'Benignus' had come through so many cruel ordeals with his faith unscathed, and getting stronger all the time. He would be particularly happy about the gentlemanly way Jim dealt with the prelates who had joined the Patriotic Church. He did not judge them and he did not condemn them. He just asked them to consider their position in the light of Catholic theology and Canon Law. After St Benignus came through his fiery ordeal unscathed, St Patrick prophesised that St Benignus would be his successor. Our Benignus, Jim Yang, was Patrick Cleary's successor in everything except in name and title, for over thirty bitter and tumultuous years. As a matter of fact, he became spokesman for the other four dioceses in the province of Jiangxi. The Reds looked on him as the leader of the loyal Catholic Church and the backbone of its resistance.

For instance, he tells us that he paid a visit to Archbishop Chou shortly after the latter was released from jail. On his way home, the Political Party Committee of Fu-Zhou, invited him to stay for a few days as their guest. In fact, he was a very special guest, because they invited him to become the Vice Chairman of the local People's Political Consultative Conference. They also promised to give him back all the Church property in Nancheng. (Fu-Zhou is in Yukiang diocese and is about halfway between Nanchang and Nancheng). They would only make him Vice Chairman of the People's Consultative Conference on one condition. The condition was that he should give the sacraments to the Patriotic Fu-Zhou Catholics, just as they were, without going through any rites of reconciliation. Jim was adamant in his refusal to accede to their request, but while Jim was in Fu-Zhou he visited as many of the loyal Catholics as he could, encouraging them and giving them hope for the future. He was in Fu-Zhou for some days during the beginning of October 1957 as far as I can make out.

In his letter, Jim goes on to say, and I quote: 'On 20 October 1957, the demons launched once again a serious combat against the Church. The previous night some of the Patriotic Church priests, backed up by police, kept us under close vigilance though we were still free to move about. But in the morning of 20 October, when I refused to come to Nanchang to attend what they called a 'meeting of study', the apostates would not let us say Mass and dragged the three of us, that is Paul Yu, Peter Hsieh and myself, into a bus which was prepared for the purpose beforehand.' Apparently Catholics, Protestants, Buddhists and Moslems would all be there at the 'meeting of study'. At the meeting, the Patriotic Church representatives attacked Jim Yang in a most hostile and resentful fashion.

They were led by a Nanfeng priest, who had joined the Patriotic Church Movement. Despite the hatred and hostility of the Patriotic people, they served him and his companions with fish on the Friday they were there. The comedy of this was not lost on Jim. He writes: 'You see how cunning the Pharisees were. They would let us keep our minor customs but would not let us stick to our faith.' During the free times between the meetings, Jim visited the loyal Catholics in Nanchang. He encouraged them not to be afraid whatever might happen and exhorted them not to worry about his safety as our Lord, and his Mother were always looking after him. Again, I quote from his letter: 'Who could deprive me of my life, I told them, if it were God's will that I should live for his glory, and it would be my glory, if I should die for my faith?'

When I read those magnificent words of Jim Yang's, I had this strong feeling of *deja vu* but, where did I see them before? Of course, in the letter of St Ignatius of Antioch to the Romans. St Ignatius was martyred in 107 AD and was St Peter's successor at Antioch. On his way to Rome, he visited different Christian communities and asked them not to pray for his safety because he wanted to die for Christ. His letters were eagerly studied by men and women who made martyrdom the main romance of this early age in the Church's history, according to Maisie Ward in her book, *Early Church Portrait Gallery*. Somehow or other, words and sentiments like those of St Ignatius of Antioch seem strangely out of place in the twentieth century. The realisation that they were written by my friend, Jim Yang, gives me an eerie feeling. Maybe God permits persecution so that we twentieth century people may catch some of the first fervour of the early Christians, when our Church was young.

Of course, I should have noted that although Jim visited the Catholics in Nanchang city and also in Fu-Zhou, his first pastoral priority was the Catholics of Nancheng diocese. When he was released in 1955 and allowed to go back to what we used to call the convent, one would have thought that he would take a good rest after three years of great hardship in jail. But Jim was not that type. He set out immediately to visit the Catholics in Nancheng diocese, and to encourage them to the best of his ability. Everywhere he went, he said Mass and gave a short sermon. In some places, the local cadres came to have a look. They were flabbergasted. They thought that the Catholic Church in Nancheng was dead and buried. He administered the sacraments to all the sick. Later, when Tommy Yu was ordained, before Easter 1957, Tommy tried to visit the Catholics in the North Line, where Pat Sheehy, Mike Halford, Luke Teng and I had been pastors. They found it very consoling that the good Catholics were so eager to see their priests.

No, Jim was not the type who would rest, though he deserved a rest, after all his sufferings in jail from February 1952 to the Spring of 1955. He tells us in his letter that he would not let a day go to waste without doing some work for the greater glory of God. On 30 April 1957, he and Paul Yu and Tommy Yu, went on a pilgrimage of gratitude to Our Lady of China. I quote from his letter: 'I said Mass on the main altar on 1 May and offered the diocese once more to Our Blessed Lady, entreating her to give us a special protection under her powerful cloak.' The Shrine is at Szo-Shan, about twenty miles from Shanghai.

Later in the year, Jim repeated that offering of the diocese to Our Lady, in Nancheng. He tells us about it in his letter:

> On the Sunday after the Feast of the Holy Rosary, I gathered all the priests and the good Catholics together, and made a solemn offering of the whole diocese of Nancheng to Our Lady, imploring her to protect us in our dangers, console us in our misery, and finally bring us to her Blessed Child Jesus when we pass from this valley of tears. Our Lady deigned to listen to our prayer, for everyone of us felt her special protection in our imprisonment, especially in our combatant life

against the demons. She has also given us consolations enough to endure whatever persecution we might suffer in the future.

Jim did not have long to wait for his next ordeal. In Jim's own words 'on the Feast of Christ the King, 29 October 1957, I lost my freedom absolutely till 29 October 1975.' Jim was in Nanchang at the time the unexpected blow fell. As I have noted, he visited and encouraged the loyal Catholics and one of them, Yu Aiju, a native of Kiutu, the parish where I had served, invited him to say Mass in her house. A good crowd came, including quite a few students. As Jim was giving out Holy Communion, a 'band of demons' as he called them came in and began to interfere with his administration of the sacrament. In his own words, 'at that time I got a bit angry and shouted, "Keep quiet as my Mass is not yet over." My stern attitude gave them a shock and they stood there just like a flock of wooden geese. Having finished my Mass and made my thanksgiving, I said, "Alright now, what do you want to do?"' He was told that the head official wanted to see him. Jim retorted. 'If the head official wants to see me, why do you come in such a big crowd as if you were going to meet a strong enemy?' He and some of his congregation were driven to the main prison, Prison No. 1, in Nanchang.

The Catholics who were arrested with Jim were released but Jim was taken to Fu-Zhou jail and was imprisoned there for one year. Then he was taken back to Nancheng jail and there he met our heroic catechist John McCormack, or to use his Chinese name, Matthias Hsu. In Nancheng, he was sentenced to twenty years imprisonment. It was a savage sentence even according to Communist standards. Jim protested and, as a Chinese lawyer, was allowed to plead his cause legally. I quote from Jim:

> I told them all the facts they used for my accusation were either fabricated ones or twisted, therefore they were null and void, and could not be used as the basis of the charges against me. Therefore the sentence should be invalid and illegal. The principal judge with whom I was quite familiar urged me to appeal to the Higher Court if I considered the judgement unfair. At first, I thought there would be no use in

appealing as 'all crows are black' (a Chinese phrase). But the man urged me again and again to do so.

Finally, I agreed to write an appeal to Fu-Zhou, the Higher Court, to refute the reason they gave for their charges against me. The Fu-Zhou Court changed some facts, but they put some other forged ones instead and kept the original judgement of Nancheng court and deprived me of my right of further appealing.

Such cases of even-handed injustice were part and parcel of the Communist so-called legal system. On 6 January 1960, Jim was sent to Nanchang. Jim continues in his letter:

Due to the terrible weakness of my poor health, I had to be sent to a hospital of the prison to get treatment the day after I arrived. The good Catholic, Dr Teng, a prisoner too, was the chief doctor of the clinic and he gave me treatment. I was absolutely dying, but under Teng's good care, my health was gradually restored. I stayed in the hospital for more than two months.

With Jim brought back to health from death's door in Nancheng prison, and ready for the new and most frightening of his ordeals, perhaps we should pause here and look back. I suggest this because I am intrigued and fascinated by Bishop Cleary's gentle question to the priests who criticised him for giving too much time to Jim Yang. The words were: 'Did not Patrick have his Benignus?' I am convinced now, after having looked through a few lives of St Patrick, that Bishop Cleary's words were not merely tinged with prophecy but they were also a declaration of intent. He was declaring that he was going to train Jim Yang in the same way as St Patrick trained St Benignus to the best of his ability. The bishop was a scholar and St Patrick was his patron and he must have read a number of lives of the saint before and after he was appointed a missionary bishop. A more successful missionary bishop than St Patrick would be hard to find in the pages of Church history, and I believe Bishop Cleary modelled himself as a bishop on St Patrick's methods in so far as the situation he found himself in would permit. As I said, the similarities between St Benignus' part in St Patrick's apostolate and Jim

Yang's part in Patrick Cleary's apostolate are striking. Just as St Benignus helped to light St Patrick's fire at Slane, when the light of faith was burning low in the parishes of Nancheng, Jim helped to fan the faith into flame by his pastoral visits and by his encouragement and by saying Mass. He held aloft his flaming torch, everywhere he went, fearlessly.

I had often wondered why Jim was sent to do Chinese Law rather than say Canon Law or theology after his ordination. But when I read *St Patrick Apostolate of Ireland* by Fr Morris, and learned that Benignus had assisted St Patrick in revising the Brehon Laws, I said audibly to myself 'Eureka! I have discovered!' I mean I took it for granted that Benignus must have some training in the Brehon Law just as Jim had training in Chinese Civil Law. Patrick Cleary was modelling his Benignus on St Patrick's Benignus. Apart from that, it was a very wise decision because Jim's knowledge of Civil Law was very helpful to him during his trials.

Even before I left for China in 1946, I met some of the Nancheng priests who were on holiday here in Navan. One of them told me that the bishop of Nancheng was a lovely bishop and that I was going to our nicest diocese in China. However, he continued, he can be a bit 'up in the air' at times. He has a young priest, Fr Jim Yang, and he has spent an awful lot of his time training him, and do you know what he said when one of the boys told him he was spoiling Jim by giving so much time to his training? He said, and you will die laughing when you hear this one, he said, 'Did not Patrick have his Benignus?' Imagine comparing Jim Yang to St Benignus, did you ever hear the like of it?

In 1946, my response was a loud statutory laugh when an older priest, especially an 'old China hand', told me something which he claimed was not only funny but also lethal. In 1995, with the gift of hindsight, my response would be, 'No, I never heard the likes of it.' The comparison between St Benignus and Jim Yang, our twentieth-century Benignus, was amazingly apt, in a sense prophetic. I marvel at how the power of the Spirit working in Jim sent him from jail out to the parishes of the diocese, confronting and confuting his persecutors like a latter day St

Columban, and bringing hope and healing and encouragement to the Catholics in these first eight years of his imprisonment. There is a danger, I suppose, that as a priest of Nancheng diocese, like Jim himself was, my evaluation of his apostolate during the eight years I have covered might be a bit fulsome. For that reason for the next twenty years, or so which Jim had to spend doing penal servitude in Nanchang No. 1 prison, I shall hand you over to another commentator, as Jim himself says very little in the letter he sent to us about this period of penal servitude.

CHAPTER 5

As Others See Us

Robbie Burns, the Scottish poet, has written:

Oh wad some power the giftie gie us,
to see ourselves as others see us.
It would frae monie a blunder free us,
And foolish notion.

Being able to see our friends as others see them, can also be a very enlightening experience as I discovered when I read an article in the Hong Kong *Sunday Examiner* of 15 February 1990. The article was entitled 'My Comrade in Arms – Fr James Yang', by She Fang. The priest who wrote it thought it prudent, even in 1990, to write under a pen name. Presumably, he felt that a Catholic newspaper like the *Sunday Examiner* would be closely scrutinised by Communist spies in Hong Kong.

She Fang starts, 'I met a priest of the same congregation as myself, and he said to me seriously and affectionately "You owe a debt to your deceased comrade in battle; you must pay it back without delay."' The writer then goes on to say that when he was given an eight year sentence in No. 1 prison, Nanchang, he heard there were four other prisoners there, one of them being Fr Jim Yang. However, he did not see any of the other four priests and to the best of my reckoning, he began his eight year sentence in 1958. Let me quote again from She Fang: 'Suddenly the government made an unexpected attack on all the priest prisoners. They brought us down to the underground water prison in No. 1 jail.' It was a horrible place and only prisoners who had committed very serious crimes were sent there.

He goes on: 'The cells of the so-called water prison were literally surrounded by water. In the middle of the cell there was a heap of cement formed in the shape of a bed which allowed two persons to sleep there. One could not see the sun or the sky. It was neither day nor night. There was only one light in the passage. Even if one were allowed a book, one could not read. There were just five small cells for five priests.'

The writer of the article goes on to say then 'that the prison warder took him to the wrong cell first. The warder discovered his mistake when they saw an old man dressed like a workman on the cement bed.' The writer did not know the old man but later he came to the conclusion that it was Jim Yang. The warder closed the door fast when he discovered that he had made a mistake. Again, I quote from the article: 'To be in the water prison was a great affliction. Night and day one had to sit on the cement bed, but it was unhealthy to sleep all day. Fortunately, except for those who came to bring us meals, nobody had any concern for us living in this underground prison.

'To pass the time, we sang sacred songs and hymns and our conversation passed from one cell to another. In this way I discovered Fr Yang there but we were not able to meet each other. We were there for forty days as it were from Lent to Easter Sunday. We too felt like people who had come out of a tomb and were able to see the sky again.' She Fang's article goes on: 'In 1974, Fr Yang and I finished our sentences and were sent to work in the brick factory in No. 4 prison. Then we were able to meet each other.' He was a fervent priest who was loyal to the Church and he had a great love of Our Lady. At that time, however, we did not have any chances to meet each other. In 1978, he was sent to work in a plastics factory and I was in the Nanchang switchgear plant, about 1 kilometer away from the plastic factory. So I used to visit him. Sometimes he would prepare a few dishes and invite me to have lunch with him. Sometimes he came to see me.

From that time we became better acquainted. He was trained by the Columban Fathers and had learned to speak English very well. He had studied law at Amoy University. He was very proficient at Chinese and at writing Chinese with a brush. He had great power of discernment, knowing very well there could be no compromise where religious matters were concerned. In 1974 he was once more sent back from No. 4 Prison to No. 1.

He was given chemical work to do (working out a formula for

making plastic) and was very successful at this work. Later he was asked to teach Chemistry. He also had to teach English to the children of the cadres in Guanbo University. People called him Yang, Sir, and respected him greatly. He had many English books and loved to study. In fact, he was extremely intellectual.'

He then goes on: 'In 1981 I returned home for a family visit but was re-arrested a month later. At the time I was arrested in Shanghai, Fr Yang was re-arrested in Nanchang. Later we were put into two different cells in Chanling Detention Prison and were put on trial separately. Later still I learned that he had fallen ill and had been sent to the labour camp hospital. He tried in every way to send me a little note in English. It went "I will be loyal to the Pope until death." He probably realised that he would not live long so he wanted to express the deep thoughts of his heart. He already knew he had cancer which was spreading through his body and which was incurable.

'The Patriotic Church Association knew Fr Yang was much respected and a very important person. If he agreed to join the Patriotic Association, there would be no problem to get other priests to join it too. Even many of the faithful would be ready to join. The Reds promised to obtain effective treatment for his illness until he was cured, if he would join the Patriotic Church, but he was immovable in this matter.

'Fr Yang was a very conscientious man and very exact in his way of life. Even when he was in prison or sick he dressed tidily and was always optimistic because he regarded death as a home coming and was never depressed. Because of his gifts, qualifications and good reputation, there was no priest in Jiangxi Province comparable to him. The government tried to persuade him to become a bishop but he preferred to die rather than become a state appointed bishop. He died at home in utter poverty. I consider myself to be very fortunate to have struggled and suffered side by side with this outstanding priest for nearly thirty years.'

Seeing Jim Yang as She Fang saw him was for us Columbans who worked with him in Nancheng, an enlightening experience.

It filled us with gratitude to God for having given us such an outstanding priest to lead our other priests and people during the long dark years of persecution. The letter showed us too how familiarity can blind us to the gifts and qualifications of our friends. Above all, it brought home to us how self-effacing Jim was in the twenty-six page letter he wrote to us in 1980. Most of the letter, you could say, was devoted to the sufferings and heroic witness of our other Chinese priests in Nancheng. He did, of course, mention his pastoral visits during periods of 'semi-freedom' to the different parishes of Nancheng because he knew of our very deep interest in these visits.

But he never mentioned a word about the 'great affliction' – the 'forty days of Lent' – in that horrible and notorious underground water prison in Nanchang No. 1 jail. When I came to that part of She Fang's letter, I thought of 'the black hole of Calcutta'. I could see the darkness not only through the night but also through the day. I felt that Jim was in the ideal place for contracting a very deep dose of depression – of the deepest and most virulent and, I believe, the most prestigious form of depression, which I understand is called 'Black Dog'.

But as I read on, I discovered that Jim did not get a dose of 'Black Dog' or indeed of the milder forms of depression. To my surprise and delight, She Fang wrote of Jim, 'He was never depressed'. I had underestimated the power of the Spirit to inoculate Jim against depression by filling him with Christian hope and Christian joy. A Chinese sage says that 'Sitting in an upright posture in silence is good without accompanying evil.' But when one is sitting on that cement bed in an evil place like the water prison for forty days and nights, as Jim was, it is not easy to share the sentiments of the sage. It must be horrible beyond words, yet She Fang writes that Jim was always optimistic, realising that death is a home-coming. Jim would have been amused when his countryman described him as very intellectual. Yet familiarity blinded us to Jim's many God-given gifts and talents. What a pleasant surprise to read in She Fang's article that Jim was given chemical work to do, 'working out a formula for making plastic', and that he was very successful at his work. So successful was he that later he was asked to teach chemistry. I did know, of course, that Jim seemed to attract intellectuals around him when he was in jail and in times of semi-freedom.

In the long letter he wrote to us Columbans in 1980, the following occurs: 'There are a good number of intellectuals especially among young people interested in Christianity. Some of them have asked me again to lend them books about Christianity. Please send such books, in Chinese, of course. I remember before liberation there used to be a book about the lives of Catholic scientists and a Chinese version of *Fabiola* (both of which I have read). If you could kindly get one or two copies of each for me I should be very grateful.' He must have often thought of *Faboiola* during the long dark years of his imprisonment when he and his fellow priests and prisoners sang sacred hymns and songs and thus kept united in mind and heart. In that dark twentieth-century catacomb in Nanchang, he must have thought of the catacombs in the early days of Christianity. *Fabiola*, written by Cardinal Wiseman, is about persecution in the early Church.

We all knew that Jim was very proficient at Chinese but when She Fang told us in the article that Jim was very proficient in painting Chinese characters with a brush – that was an unexpected revelation. Let Lin Yutang, the Chinese scholar, tell us about it. He writes in *My Country and My People*: 'Calligraphy has been elevated to the true level of an art on a par with Chinese paintings. Calligraphy and painting are regarded as sister arts and calligraphy has the wider appeal.'

I have an example of Chinese calligraphy which was given to me by Joe Flynn, a friend of mine since our days in Nancheng diocese together. It is a scroll nearly five feet long on which clusters of Chinese characters are painted with a brush, starting at the bottom, it seems. It conveys to me the impression of clusters of birds in flight upwards. It conveys to me the impression of movement, rhythm and it has a beauty I cannot easily describe. But then it has been noted that beauty is in the eye of the beholder. I had no idea that Jim had an artistic gift of this nature. We all knew that, as a priest, Jim was fervent, exemplary and deeply committed, but we are very grateful to She Fang for telling us so much about Jim Yang the man. We are grateful to him for telling us so much about his talents and versatility which we had not noticed or had taken for granted.

However, the most moving item of information given to us by She Fang was about the little note which Jim wrote to him in English. The message was brief and it went 'I will be loyal to the Pope till death'. Bishop Patrick Cleary must have frequently reminded Jim of St Patrick's exhortation to his spiritual children: 'As you are of Christ, so be also of Rome.' Jim, in his letter to us, quoted a saying from the early Church: 'Where Peter (the Pope) is, there is the Church.' For over thirty years, Jim had passed on this message to his fellow Catholics in jail and during his periods of semi-freedom to the people in the various parishes and mission stations of the diocese. So it was fitting this should be his last message to this comrade in battle to whom we are indebted for this tribute to Jim. We are indebted to She Fang for saving us from the blunder of underestimating Jim's gifts, his talents, his spirit of joyful hope, all through the persecution.

CHAPTER 6

Faithful to Christ and to Rome

But Jim Yang did not confine himself in telling Catholic and Communist alike that he would be loyal to the Pope till death. He did more. He communicated his sentiments, 'the deep thought of his heart', as She Fang called it, to Pope John Paul II himself.

It happened like this. In the twenty-six page letter Jim wrote to us in 1980, the following occurs. 'If you get the opportunity, please send a report to His Holiness for us. Let the Holy Father know that, though small and unknown to fame as our diocese is, there are in it four priests fighting bravely for their faith; they have refused to join the Patriotic Church at the loss of their freedom for more than twenty-five years. In fact, five of their comrades have already given their lives for the same cause. I want you to do this for me, not because we have anything worthy to make a boast of. But we wish to let the Holy See know that we are not unworthy to be children of St Columban's and that the apostolic work of our most respected and beloved Bishop Cleary has definitely brought forth its fruit. We wish finally to let the Holy Father know that we are still keeping on fighting for the loyalty to the Papacy, so we beg this special blessing and prayers that we will stand sternly till we get a triumphant victory of our Holy Mother Church.'

Jim asked the late Ted MacElroy, our man in Hong Kong, to send a copy of the letter to Seamus O'Reilly and a copy to me. Ted also sent a copy to our Procurator General in Rome, Bill Halliden. Bill very kindly typed Jim's letter, which was in longhand. He then sent a typed copy of Jim's letter to Archbishop Achille Silvestrini, Secretary to the Council for Public Affairs of the Church. In his letter to the archbishop, Bill has the following: 'I have given a copy of this letter to Archbishop Loudarsamy of the Sacred Congregation for the Evangelisation of Peoples, with the request that a report be given to his Holiness, John Paul II, as Fr Yang so earnestly desires.' Bill's letter was dated 4 April 1981.

In his reply, dated 2 July 1981, Archbishop Silvestrini ends his letter by saying, 'I thank you very much for sending me the document which I have perused with great interest and attention.' Yes, it would be of the greatest interest for the archbishop to receive a letter written, not only by an observer or China-watcher in Hong Kong, but from a priest who had suffered for thirty years in the fiery furnace of the Red persecution. The persecution was still going strong when Jim, in his own words, had seized the opportunity of writing during a period of semi freedom. Archbishop Silvestrini was in charge of the Church's diplomatic relationships with civil governments. Since the expulsion of the Nuncio in 1951, the Holy See had no diplomatic ties with Red China.

Jim's letter gave the archbishop very clear information regarding the attitude of the Red government to the Catholic Church in the province of Jiangxi. It is fair to conclude that the Chinese government's attitude to the Church in the other thirty-five provinces was substantially the same. From Archbishop Silvestrini's point of view, you could say that Jiangxi was China in miniature.

The archbishop must have found Jim's letter a heart warming report. It told of the diocese where all the priests remained faithful to the Pope despite tremendous pressures by the Reds to make them join the Patriotic Church. But that was only half it. It also told how Jim Yang, the Vicar General of the diocese, wrote letters to fifty prelates, bishops and archbishops, who had been pressurised into joining the Patriotic Church. It told how Jim had written to them to ask them to consider their positions in the light of Canon Law and Catholic theology.

The letter was timely as well. Archbishop Silvestrini got it in April 1981. After President Nixon's visit to China early in 1972, there was an outbreak of what has been called 'China Fever' amongst evangelical groups, liberal Christians and missionaries in the USA. It soon spread to Europe. The late Fr Laslo Ladany SJ, our foremost authority on the Catholic Church in Red China, describes the 'China Fever' in his book, *The Catholic Church in China*, written in 1987. Fr Ladany was a Jesuit who was born in Hungary but lived in China from 1940-1949. From 1953 to 1982, he published a weekly newsletter called 'China News Analysis'. Here is what he says about the China Fever:

> The image of China the Wonderful, the ideal country and ideal society, mesmerized a great part of the world including many Christians. In the turbulent years of the 70s many in the Western world had a deep longing for an ideal society, and felt impelled to project the image of such a place somewhere. This mirage deeply affected Christian thinking about China. China was described not as a country that has exterminated Christianity, together with all other religions, a country ruled by atheists under proletarian dictatorship, a country where there was no trace of freedom of the press, or expression of personal opinions, but as a country where Christian virtues flourish, a country to which the Christian world can look at as a model; a country with a social system that needs only some correctives to become true realisation of God's Kingdom on earth.

Tony Lambert, Consultant of the Overseas Missionary Fellowship, Hong Kong, who has lived in Beijing for some time, quotes Ladany's words with approval in his book, *Resurrection of the Chinese Church*. The book was written in 1990. He notes that the illusions cherished by many people in the 70s, and described by Ladany, are applicable in the 1990s. The illusions are cherished because people accept the masterful propaganda of the Patriotic Church at its face value. He adds that secular journalists were too realistic to swallow the Red propaganda. Missionaries on their way home from other mission fields visited China and did a spot of China-watching for a week or two. They visited the places the Red wanted them to visit and saw the sights which the Reds wanted them to see. Perhaps because of this, some of them caught the 'China Fever'.

While one can understand individual missionaries catching the disease, it is a bit more difficult to understand how two prestigious organisations like the Lutheran World Federation of Geneva and the *Pro Mundi Vita*, a Brussels based Catholic organisation, could have become infected. They had an ecumenical meeting in Louvain in September 1974. Here is how Fr Ladany SJ summarises their conclusion in his book: 'In short, the image of Communist China is projected as a pioneer in Christian experience of the fulfilment of God's will of salvation on earth paving the way to the realisation of a millenium'.

The Sacred Congregation for the Public Affairs of the Church, and the Sacred Congregation for the Evangelisation of Peoples, would have to take note of the conclusions of such prestigious bodies as those meeting in Louvain. Jim's letter, written from the battle front so to speak, would have provided the Sacred Congregations with a balanced corrective to the wishful thinking of the China experts in Europe and America. For thirty years he had denounced the false teachings and propaganda of the Communists by word and deed in China; now his letter was providing the Roman congregation with ammunition to battle against that same propaganda throughout the universal Church.

We old China hands were very amused reading about the land of bondage we had left twenty years earlier now being presented to the world as 'Paradise Regained'. We had underestimated the ability of the Reds as propagandists. They realised the axiom stated in the funny book *The Peter Principle* – 'An ounce of image is worth a pound of performance'. We roared with laughter when a couple of our missionaries visiting China for a couple of weeks to do a spot of China-watching came up with remarks like the following: 'There is something transcendent here (in China's Communism).' Another remark from a China-watcher was 'whether one joined the Patriotic Church or not is irrelevant'. Jim Yang, who suffered so much for the faith we brought him, would have laughed heartily too because he had a great sense of humour. Jim would have said that it was essential for the China-watcher to remember that the Church he was shown was not the real Church.

Tony Lambert tells us that some liberal Christians in 1990, a year after Tienanmen, still cherish the illusion that China is a country to which the Christian world can look to as a model. One would have thought that the massacre, the repression at Tienanmen, would have cured everybody of 'China Fever' for ever. Perhaps Pushkin, the Russian writer, has a point when he notes, 'the illusion that exalts us is dearer then ten thousand truths'.

I sometimes think that the motto of the China Patriotic Church propagandists may have been, 'Let us look after the China-watchers and our image will look after itself.' Be this as it may, people like Dick Hillis of Los Angeles boosted the Red image immensely by a book he edited in 1972. The book was entitled, *The Sayings of Mao Tse Tung and the Sayings of Jesus*. The book favourably compared quotations from Mao and from Jesus on the same or similar subjects. But the new China image-makers were not confined to the States. A similar book entitled, *The Thoughts of Mao Tse Tung*, appeared in this part of the world and students began to read it fairly avidly. But it all seemed so remote from my little world until I got a letter from the President of St Jarlath's, Tuam, the late Mgr Mooney, who at Archbishop Cunnane's suggestion invited me to give a talk to the students of my old boarding school. I burst out laughing when I saw the subjects on which I was expected to talk – 'The Thoughts of Mao Tse Tung'!

Apparently a number of the students were reading the book enthusiastically and catching , or in danger of catching, the 'China Fever'. I laughed so loudly when I got the invitation because it seemed to me that the wheel had gone full circle. I had left St Jarlath's College to bring the good news of Christianity, the thoughts of Jesus Christ, to the poor people in China. Two years and a half after my arrival there, I bumped into the Chinese Peoples Army of Liberation whose leader was Mao Tse Tung. They informed us that they were bringing the good news of Marxism as understood by Mao Tse Tung to the poor people of China. Their aim was, they said, to liberate the Chinese people from the oppression of the landlords and the Nationalist Party inside China and from superstitions like religion which had been brought to China by missionaries like us. Karl Marx had

FAITHFUL TO CHRIST AND TO ROME 55

said that religion is 'the opium of the people' and their leader, Mao Tse Tung, regarded us missionaries as 'running dogs' for imperialism and colonialism.

The Chinese Communists harassed us as criminals and hounded us out of the country. Now, twenty years later, I found the long arm of the Communist propaganda was following me across the planet to my place of origin. In China the Communists had accused me of sabotaging the revolution. Now I found myself invited to sabotage the Communist propaganda contained in the 'Thought of Mao Tse Tung' and to debrief those who were brainwashed by it. Karl Marx had said that history repeats itself twice, first as tragedy, and then as comedy. For me, the Red China experience was the tragedy. Visiting St Jarlath's to treat an outbreak of 'China Fever' was the comedy – from my point of view.

I cannot remember exactly what I said to the boys. My impression is that I told them their interest in the 'Thoughts of Mao Tse Tung' showed that they were compassionate young men who were dismayed at the injustice in the world of the 70s. In the Third World, thousands of children were dying each day through lack of food or shelter. It was natural that they should admire Mao Tse Tung because he set out to get rid of the injustice in China. He tried and shot the landlords with the object of giving the land to the poor peasants. Inflation was, eventually, brought under control, roads were improved in many parts of the country, the people had more to eat, bandits and beggars disappeared.

On the other hand, it should be said that in 1951 he invaded Tibet and, after much bloodshed, took over the country. He had no more right to do this than the colonists and imperialists had to take over parts of China. He shot the people whom he described as landlords in the village where I was pastor, and wiped out millions of others throughout the vast country, but the poor did not get the land. The land was taken over by the army. In other places, collectivisation took place.

In 'The Thoughts of Mao Tse Tung', we read that when injustices and inefficiency were put right, the state would fade away and a classless society would emerge. But in China, when I was living there, the state did not fade away. In fact, it became a police state. Freedom faded away. Even freedom to think. The people were expected to listen daily on the radio to the thoughts of Mao Tse Tung in order that the thoughts might be put into action.

Communists do not believe in God. The worship we give him, they regard as superstition. But they believed in personality cult in China – the personality to which they accorded cult or worship being Mao Tse Tung. The 'helmsman' himself, Mao Tse Tung, seemed to like it and encourage it. One of the most striking of Mao Tse Tung's thoughts to be found in the little red book is 'Political power flows out of the mouth of a gun'. To such an extent did Mao Tse Tung's political power grow out of the mouth of a gun that after his victory in 1949 Mao Tse Tung exterminated his political opponents, the Nationalists. Landlords were also exterminated. Between landlords and Nationalists, some millions were exterminated and many more millions were sent to slave labour camps.

But Mao Tse Tung believed in being a good Marxist. Now according to Frank Sheed, in his book, *Communism and Man*, Marxism was the first great movement in history whose object was to help the poor and downtrodden which made *hate* the principle of progress. So in 1966, Mao Tse Tung started the cultural revolution. He decided it was time to stoke up the fires of hatred again, because he believed revolution must be ongoing. The cultural revolution which started in 1966 was the most savage phase of the Red Revolution in China. It resulted in the closure of all churches as well as Buddhist temples and, most surprisingly, put an end to Muslim temples and other shrines. It forbade external manifestations of religious beliefs. Church buildings were turned into markets, schools, and other non-religious purposes. The cultural revolution was going on at the time I was speaking to the boys. Although we did not have Jim Yang's letter until 1980, Fr Tommy Yu sent short messages to Hong Kong where his sister, Sr Teresita Yu, received them and passed them on to Fr Seamus O'Reilly and to myself. We got, from her, an outline of what Jim later gave us in great detail in his letter. The objective of the cultural revolution was to destroy the 'four olds', old culture, old customs, old ideas, and old habits, according to Mao Tse Tung.

So, Communism as described in *The Thoughts of Mao Tse Tung*, is not a cure for the injustice of unbridled capitalism and exploitation of labour, which we find in the world of the 90s. The reason is that it destroys and it forbids freedom of opinion, freedom of assembly, freedom of franchise, freedom of worship. It is not a recipe for founding a brotherhood of man, because it is based on hatred and ongoing hatred. Certain of the more obvious evils of Capitalism would be destroyed by Communism but too much else would be destroyed with them.

Let Frank Sheed have the last word. In his book, *Communism and Man*, he declares that Communism is the cure for inequality and injustice, very much in the sense in which P.G. Wodehouse says that 'the guillotine is a cure for dandruff'. What was of permanent value and free from errors in the writings of Karl Marx is preserved in *Rerum Novarum* and in the other Catholic Encyclicals on social justice since then. In fairness to Marx, I should say that his Communist manifesto in 1847 alerted us to our duties to the poor, the oppressed, the exploited workers and it helped to clarify the industrial problems of the day. It came about forty-five years before Pope Leo XIII wrote his Encyclical, *Rerum Novarum*.

I told the boys that every country has agencies for helping development in the Third World and for generating an awareness in Catholics of their duties to get involved in this work. There is another agency in every country which is concerned with human rights, at home and abroad. 'Your interest in the thoughts of Mao Tse Tung shows your compassion and concern for the injustices and inequalities of the world. I suggest you get involved in one of the agencies I have mentioned and, by doing so, you can play a part in liberating people from injustice, exploitation, oppression. Communism does not bring such liberation. My fellow missionaries and I suffered from 'Communist Liberation' twenty years ago and I still suffer what I would like to call 'Liberation lag'.

Communism does not work. To revert to Frank Sheed's comparison, it is a most effective dandruff destroyer, but the price is too high. I hope I finished with a story I like to tell about the personality cult accorded to Mao Tse Tung even away back in the 50s. At that time the cult had scarcely got off the ground. In my district I noticed that all the Communist bosses were Northerners. They conscripted young men in the locality to help them, and gave them jobs. Some of the young men were more careerist than Communist. A sure-fire way of getting promotion in the job was to be able to make a very eloquent speech plugging the Party line and denouncing the local landlord. The formula for ending such speeches never varied. The young orator, when he finished his speech, would bow to the Commissar and then bow to the people and then declaim the formula 'If I have said anything good, let the praise go to Mao Tse Tung; if I have said anything wrong, let the head be swept off me'. I trust the final sentence of my talk was, 'If I have said anything good, let the praise go to God, if I have said anything wrong, let the dandruff be swept off me.'

Red China propaganda peaked in the early 70s. After the death of Mao Tse Tung in 1976, it began to wane a little, and reading *The Thoughts of Mao Tse Tung* gradually went out of fashion. My diagnosis was that the boys in St Jarlath's were for the most part following the fashion rather than catching the 'China Fever'. A few, no doubt, would have caught 'the fever'; they would have been influenced by Irish card-holding Communists. The party was well organised in this country though numerically small. I remember when Bishop Cleary and Seamus O'Reilly were being tried as criminals in Nancheng on 8 February 1952, the Communist Party here sent the Nancheng Reds a telegram. They wished them well in their efforts to bring us Irish criminals to justice. One of the symptoms of the 'China Fever' is gravity. I thought I detected a little unexpected gravity in some of the St Jarlath's boys. Unexpected because I always think of St Jarlath's as a dwelling place of laughter and levity, in my time there.

So Jim did his bit to counter Communist propaganda abroad by the messages he sent to Seamus and to me through Sr Teresita Yu in Hong Kong. Tommy Yu, another of our Nancheng priests, sent us similar messages during his periods of semi-freedom. Shortly before his death, on 29 November 1988, Jim sent another message to the Pope. Seamus O'Reilly and Tommy Murphy, a younger Columban working in Taiwan, went to Nancheng in October 1988. The main object of Seamus's visit was to see Jim Yang.

When Seamus was refused permission to visit Jim Yang, Jim cried bitterly. Seamus was deeply disappointed. Commenting on the refusal, Seamus quotes Tacitus: 'People hate those whom they have wronged.' The Reds wronged and hated Jim to his death. Jim, however, managed to send a message, through Yu Thung Gee, a Kiutu Catholic, to Seamus and Tommy Murphy.

Jim asked that Seamus and Tommy in relaying his experience in China to Rome, stress the following points:

1. I, Fr Yang, did not at any time betray my Faith, nor did I participate in activities outside the Church.

2. During my thirty years of struggle, I firmly believed in the Papacy. I did not compromise this despite the trials I encountered because of my beliefs. I suffered whippings in prison while being suspended in the air. They wanted me to join their organisation, i.e. The Patriotic Church, but I flatly refused and remained firmly loyal to the Pope. And I want the Pope to know this as it would mean a great deal to me.

It meant a great deal to the Pope when he received the message and he was deeply moved and sent a message to the Nancheng Catholics. Jim had again taken to heart St Patrick's words to his converts: 'As you are of Christ, be you of Rome.' Tommy Murphy relayed Jim's message to the Pope through Monsignor Biggio, Chargé d'Affaires in Taipei, Taiwan. The letter was dated 23 December 1988.

Yu Thung Gee, when he had given Jim's message to Seamus and Tommy Murphy, added two sentences. 'His one wish is that Fr O'Reilly and Fr Murphy convey his message to Rome. He hopes that you will not fail to carry out his death wish and thus enable him to die in peace.' For that reason they also sent his message to Bill Halliden, our Procurator in Rome. Bill sent the message to the Secretariat of State in the Vatican. He had a letter back dated 15 December 1988. It goes as follows:

> Dear Fr Halliden,
>
> I am writing to assure you that the Holy Father has personally read the Memorandum which you presented concerning the situation of Fr James P. Yang. His Holiness wishes to convey to Fr Yang his profound sentiments of esteem and appreciation for the fidelity he has maintained over the years to the Catholic Faith in spiritual communion with the successor of Peter. With affection, His Holiness sends his Apostolic Blessing.

The letter is signed 'E. Cassidy. Substitute.'

I was thrilled to learn that the Pope had read Jim's message personally. Maybe I was a bit envious too, because, I bet you, if I wrote a letter to the Pope it would not get past the Swiss Guards. Jim, our Benignus, had come a long way since his busted romance, Chinese style, at the ripe old age of ten. Jim also gave Yu Thung Gee a photograph of himself for Seamus and Tommy Murphy. It is the last picture we have of him and it not only tells a story, but two stories. In the picture, Jim is carrying, believe it or not, an Irish blackthorn stick. Seamus explains the symbolism of the blackthorn like this:

In the tripartite life of St Patrick, we are told that the measuring of the site of the Church at Armagh was done by Patrick, who carried the 'Baculum Jesu' (*Bacall Íosa* in the Irish, Crozier of Jesus in English) in his hand. It was supposed to have been given to Patrick by Jesus himself. St Benignus would have got it from St Patrick because he succeeded him as Bishop of Armagh. Seamus goes on, 'I suggest this is what is symbolised by Fr Yang's carrying the Irish blackthorn stick, the shepherd's staff, which Bishop Patrick Cleary gave his Benignus.' Patrick Cleary was a man of signs and symbols as I shall show in a later chapter. By sign, he was saying to Jim, I am giving you what Patrick gave to his Benignus, a symbol of the pastoral authority I am vesting in you, in so far as I am able. Jim, in the picture he sent to Seamus, is also speaking in sign language. The disciple had learned the language from his master. Pictured with the blackthorn in his right hand, he is saying to all of us Columbans who have laboured in Nancheng, 'Mission accomplished. I have accomplished the work of Bishop Cleary assigned to me when he gave me this *Baculus*.' There was a touch of drama in that final salute of Jim's which Patrick Cleary would have loved.

The second story the picture tells me is this: in that picture I see Jim as a 'man of sorrows'. Remember he had no painkilling drugs, just herbal treatment for the cancer which he contacted five or six years earlier. Yu Thung Gee told Seamus and Tommy Murphy, 'He now has pain all over his body. He is suffering from liver cancer, skin cancer and kidney cancer. These three cancers are rapidly progressing and destroying him. The worst pain he suffers is from the liver cancer, although the kidney cancer is also giving him intense pain. The skin condition causes major irritation and he suffers from a very severe itch.' The cumulative effect of all the pains in the different organs since he first contracted cancer is seen to show through his eyes – through his sad tormented brown almond eyes. Etched on the crowfoot lines in the face I can see the tension, the terror, the traumas of over thirty years which Jim spent in Communist jails. To me, the snapshot told everything that a camera can tell. But the camera cannot tell all. I shall leave it to Yu Thung Gee who brought Jim's message to Seamus and Tommy Murphy to supplement the information which the camera gives to me. I quote: 'His condition is medically hopeless and he is offering all his unbearable suffering to Christ and will carry his cross to the very end. Despite all, he has no regrets and carries the cross with willingness and joy.'

A Chinese sage has said, 'Without sorrow none will become Buddhas'. Buddha means 'enlightened one'. The heavy burden of sorrow and pain which he had to bear no doubt played its part in making him an enlightened leader. Another Chinese saying is, 'Only with cutting is jade shaped to use; only with adversity does man achieve to wisdom.' The trials and traumas that he bore shaped him into the instrument God wanted and used very effectively over the years. Still, that last picture of Jim frightens me and reminds me of all the famous paintings of 'The

Man of Sorrows' which I have seen. It is not the picture of Jim which I want to keep for the files of memory. The picture of him I want to always remember I shall show you shortly.

CHAPTER 7

A Picture to Remember

To show you the picture I keep of Jim Yang in the picture album of memory, let us travel back on the 'wings of the morning' a journey of forty-nine years to Nancheng, December 1946. Five of us young Columbans, John O'Doherty, Frank Ruddy, Jim Donohue, Maurice McNiffe and I arrived in Nancheng on the 3 November, the Feast of St Francis Xavier, Patron of the Missions. One could not ask for a better day on which to arrive than the feast of this great missionary saint.

A few days after our arrival, Jim Yang showed us around the Catholic compound in Nancheng. It was a large plant including a hospital, dispensary, seminary, orphanage, old people's home, convent and primary school, cathedral and bishop's house.

Jim was three years ordained and he looked very young and joyful and healthy and hopeful. He spoke perfect English but slowly and with a slight touch of the 'brogue'. He was full of witticisms and laughter, pulling back the sleeves of his cassock now and then, as he gestured dramatically. We five Columbans were round about the same age as Jim and for us too the world was young.

The bishop's house had too storeys. On the first, you had the bursar's office, the refectory, and about five bedrooms. Halfway through the house, opposite the front door, a stone stairway took you to the upstairs rooms which included an oratory, the bishop's room and office, and a few bedrooms. As one came down the stairs to the ground floor, the front door, generally closed, was straight in front of you. There was a fairly wide open space like a hotel foyer between the bottom of the stairs and the front door. It was the coolest part of the house in the summer.

The Chinese called it the *chongh ha* and we played cards in the *chongh ha* when we came for a short vacation in the summer. It was easy to see that Jim was a very good storyteller, and he liked to provide us with dramatic surprises. As we reached the *chongh ha* he told us to come towards the front door, then he told us to stand there facing the stairs across from the *chongh ha*. 'You know', he said, 'when the Japanese captured Nancheng in 1942, the orphan girls in the compound were terrified. They feared they would be raped by the Japanese. They had good reason to be terrified and so a number of them took refuge in the *chongh ha* of the bishop's house, right here. However, a Japanese soldier followed them and pointed his rifle at them ordering them out of the house to a destination somewhere in the city.

Just as the soldier pointed his rifle, Tom Ellis, who was then the administrator of the cathedral, came out of his room, stood in front of the pointed rifle and started to parley with the soldier. The soldier got furious and was about to pull the trigger when who comes down the stairs but the bishop? When the latter saw what was happening, he pushed Tom Ellis aside and stood in front of the loaded rifle.' He (Jim) began to speak faster as he got more excited and continued: 'Tom Ellis pushed the bishop out of the way again. In this manner they kept jostling each other. The Japanese soldier seemed to get confused and went on his way leaving the orphans unharmed. He must have found it difficult to understand how these two tall foreign missionaries were prepared to die, to protect the Chinese women.' I remember how heartily Jim laughed as he came to this part of the story and kept repeating about how the bishop and Tom Ellis pushed each other around.

Well that is the downstairs story. I had forgotten that there was an upstairs story as well, till Maurice McNiffe, who was with us that day, reminded me of it two years ago. Now that my memory has been 'jogged, I shall hand over to Jim and let him tell the upstairs story. After he led us up the stairs, Jim turned right and went into the first room on the right. It was the bishop's oratory. We knelt for a minute to adore Our Lord in the Blessed Sacrament. Then Jim stood up and pointed to the wall, behind the tabernacle in that little oratory. He said in a whisper as he

A PICTURE TO REMEMBER

pointed, 'You see a mark on that wall near where it meets the ceiling?' We said we did. 'Do you know what that mark is?' he asked us smiling, as he whetted our curiosity. 'Let me tell you. It is a bullet hole.' He then proceeded to tell us how a bullet got into that most unlikely of places – the wall of a bishop's oratory. It appears that a few drunken Japanese soldiers were on the rampage in Nancheng this particular day soon after they took over the city. So terrified were the women and the girls in the orphanage that they came over to the bishop's house, and the bishop asked the Columban Sisters to come over too. Tom Ellis and the bishop then asked all the women to go into the bishop's oratory.

The two men stood at the door on guard. Soon the slurred voices of the drunken soldiers could be heard coming up the stairs and along the corridor. When the first soldier saw the women huddled together in the oratory, he told the bishop that he and his companions had come to take the women with them. He demanded to be allowed to enter the oratory. The bishop refused. In a drunken fury the soldier raised his rifle to his shoulder and aimed point blank at the bishop's head. As he put his finger on the trigger, Tom Ellis, with great presence of mind, struck the barrel of the rifle with his open hand in an upward direction so that the aim was diverted. The bullet grazed the bishop's head, went through the top of the high doorway and landed high on the wall of the oratory behind the tabernacle. Strange to say, the report of the rifle shot seemed to sober up the soldier somewhat. He and his companions went down the stairs and left the bishop's house without causing any more trouble.

The bishop, according to Jim, always said that Tom Ellis saved his life that day and saved the women from the brutal soldiers. Afterwards, they extracted the bullet from the wall, and the bishop kept it as a kind of relic. 'You know', continued Jim, 'that the Nancheng Catholics believe that Tom Ellis is a saint.' They pray to him all the time and two Catholic women claim to have been cured from incurable ailments through his intercession. The bishop and all the priests also think that Tom Ellis was a saint. You did not know him! He died only a year ago, last March.'

Jim told us this chunk of history in story form. He told it with humour, adding Chinese sayings or proverbs here and there. He told it with enthusiasm, because the story was about the two men he most admired, and who had the biggest influence on his priestly life. Patrick Cleary, because he was Jim's teacher and friend, and Jim was his disciple, his Benignus; Tom Ellis, because he was a saint, in the estimation of the Nancheng Christian community. Saints not only influence. They also inspire. Tom Ellis' life inspired not only Jim Yang, but all the other Chinese priests who witnessed so heroically during the persecution, years later.

So that is the picture of Jim I shall always keep. Laughter on his lips, his brown almond eyes aglow with admiration for the two men who figured prominently in his story. If I close my eyes and peer across the chasm of the years, I can see Jim as he was that December morning when all the world was young. I can see his typically animated Chinese gestures and his frequent jokes as he showed us around the Catholic compound and whetted our interest in the life and holiness of Tom Ellis. I know that is how I shall see him again, when he is showing us around 'the halls of heaven' when we have reached 'Tír na nÓg', the land of the ever young.

On that December morning in 1946, it seems to me that Jim Yang dropped his voice and began to speak more slowly when he talked of Tom Ellis the saint. He chose his words carefully, like a man who has weighed the evidence. The lawyer had taken over from the storyteller. While he was talking of Tom's heroism in saving the bishop's life and defending the Nancheng women, Jim spoke rapidly and excitedly. When telling us of Tom's sanctity, he was calm, his speech was deliberate, like a lawyer weighing the evidence and presenting his case to the jury.

We Columbans who arrived in Nancheng in 1946, got the strong impression that Tom's life and death had a very profound influence on the Nancheng Catholics. Amongst the Catholics I include the seminarians, who were in the Nancheng seminary when Tom was administrator in Nancheng Cathedral. He was administrator of the Cathedral from 1938 until his death in 1945.

A PICTURE TO REMEMBER

I am indebted to Con O'Connell for his story about Tom during Tom's days as administrator in the Cathedral. Whenever Tom was going away for a week or more to visit the mission stations in the parish, he put up a notice in his room in Nancheng. The notice was for the benefit of priests coming in from the country parishes, who might need rooms for a few nights. The notice read: 'You are welcome to my room but please do not bring my itch with you. It is rather contagious.' Tom suffered, like many others in the Nancheng area, from a painful irritating and contagious itch.

Our seven Chinese priests and John McCormack, all of whom witnessed with such heroism during the persecution, were all associated with Tom in one way or another when he was administrator. John McCormack was his catechist, Fr John Chang was his curate, the priests Phil Chou and Luke Teng were in the diocese, and knew him well during this time. Jim Yang was in the seminary while Tom was in the parish. The four younger priests, who gave such outstanding witness during the persecution were Joseph Peng, who was tortured, and Tommy Yu, Peter Hsieh and Joseph Wu who each did about thirty years in jail. As young seminarians, they would have seen Tom Ellis at work and prayer in Nancheng, because they all lived in the same compound. When they first got to know him they were rather young, and their minds were impressionable, so that his apostolate would have a greater influence on them than on older Catholics.

Each of these I have mentioned, and indeed many others, caught something from Tom Ellis. I venture to think it was not his itch they caught. It has been said holiness is caught not taught. Each of them caught it in varying degrees from Tom. We go out to preach the gospel to the non-believers not only with our lips, but also with our lives. Example is the best sermon, and Tom's example was most edifying and inspiring. For all these reasons, the story of the Red persecution in Nancheng diocese will be incomplete unless the Tom Ellis factor is taken into account and put into context.

As Jim Yang told us, the Nancheng Catholics prayed to Tom

Ellis. When the persecution started they began to go to his grave to pray, to pray that God, through the intercession of Tom Ellis, would strengthen them when their faith and their Church were under attack. This story is about Catholic resistance during the persecution in Nancheng. To what extent Tom Ellis was involved in that resistance only God knows. However, the following profile of Tom may give us an inkling. It may also give us an idea of why the Nancheng Catholics continued to pray at Tom's grave in defiance of the Communists, and for years after all the Columbans had left China.

The profile of Tom will be given by the bishop, sisters and priests, who worked with him. They saw his life as a prolonged uphill struggle to become a saint. With the evidence made available to us, we can judge whether Tom Ellis, the priest, the Columban missionary, the pastor and 'watchman for God in Nancheng', reached the heights of holiness. As we reflect on the evidence we may be encouraged to imitate him in his uphill struggle, as we are all called to holiness in accordance with our state in life.

My role shall be that of casual commentator. Believe it or not I never laid an eye on Tom, until he was six and a half years well and truly dead. And do you know what I caught him at? I caught him red handed collaborating with us in our Catholic resistance movement. I shall tell you about the incident when you have read all about Tom's ascent to holiness with a song often on his lips, and light-heartedness in his humour.

CHAPTER 8

A Saint of our own

So now that Benignus has introduced us to Tom Ellis, I shall hand over to Patrick Cleary to tell us more about him. The bishop had a somewhat similar relationship with Tom as he had with Jim Yang later. He taught Tom in the first Columban seminary, St Columban's, Dalgan Park, Galway. As well as being Tom's professor he was also his rector in the seminary. Patrick Cleary and Tom Ellis both went to Nancheng in 1931. Of Tom's fourteen years in Nancheng diocese, eleven of them were in Nancheng parish where he lived in the bishop's house.

Tom died on 8 March 1945 and here is what the bishop wrote after Tom's death to the then Superior General, Dr Michael O'Dwyer. I quote: 'I suppose I should condole with you and the Society upon the loss of Fr Ellis, but I cannot find it in my heart to do so. Tom always sympathised with the Church rather than with the scholars in his translation of *Pretiosa in conspectu Domini mors Sanctorum ejus*' (which means in English 'Precious in the eyes of the Lord is the death of his saints'). He could see nothing grievous in the death of a saint and now that he is gone leaving a void that cannot be filled, I feel more inclined to rejoice in his bliss, than mourn over his loss. I can say with all sincerity that I never saw so many tears shed at the death of anybody. But there was more of happiness than loneliness in these tears for we, one and all, believe we have a saint of our very own, watching over us and with us, screaming for help in our need, and encouraging us in the fight – if we would but look, as he himself liked to think the 'people in Heaven' were doing.'

That is the bishop of the diocese speaking, and his words are recorded in the September 1945 *Far East*. He is asserting that he and the different strata of the local Christian community of which he is leader are one in mind and heart in believing that Tom Ellis was a saint. The bishop happened to be a theologian and a scholar. He knew that our present complex process of beatification only came into force under Pope Urban XIII, 1623-1644. Before that, Donald Attwater, something of an authority in this field, tells us in his *Dictionary of the Saints* that the public honouring of a holy man or woman was sanctioned in various ways, by the bishop, or a council, or a pope. In the case of the earliest saints, by the universal agreement of the local Church.

The Bishop of Nancheng did not in any way sanction the 'honouring' of Tom Ellis. The ordinary Catholics of Nancheng started to venerate him and pray to him. They venerated him by visiting his grave to beg favours through his intercession. Two women claimed to have been cured of incurable diseases through his intercession. One of them I knew well – she was the wife of the bishop's houseboy. The other I forget. I am not sure how many doctors vouched for the authenticity of the cures. Dr Yeh, a Chinese doctor who qualified in the Jesuit Aurora University in Shanghai, and Dr Otta Homberger, a German Lutheran doctor who also worked in the Catholic Hospital in Nancheng and was a great friend and admirer of Tom Ellis, I should think. Probably Fr Frank McDonald, a Glasgow Columban, who had been a doctor before he became a priest. (He had been a friend and fellow student of A.J. Cronin, the novelist and *The Keys of the Kingdom*, written by Cronin, has been dedicated to Frank.)

Yes, it was the laity who started to honour Tom and to pray to him. When I was able to understand them, I discovered that their testimony about Tom's holiness was very impressive indeed. I discovered something else. The Chinese Catholics were very impressed by the fact that Our Lord had called all of them to holiness. 'Be ye holy as your Heavenly Father is holy' he had said. Never have I heard the words 'holiness', 'saint' and 'fervour' used as frequently as in the parish where I was pastor in China. I attributed this to the Buddhist strain in the Chinese character or, if you will, the Chinese psyche. Buddhism stresses the vanity of this world and the shortness of this life. 'Life is like a candle in the wind' is a graphic Chinese expression of this mentality. I noticed, too, that they expected their priests to show them the way to holiness by their example, their prayer life, their preaching and their work. It was their testimony that Tom in these four areas was for them 'a burning and shining light', a priest carrying a flaming torch.

It seems Tom was before his time in encouraging the laity to answer Our Lord's call to holiness. The Second Vatican Council devotes a document to the laity and tells them how to make 'progress in holiness'. Tom would be a kindred spirit to that American pastor who, preaching to his people after Vatican II, said: 'All you good people are called to be saints: it does not matter what your state in life is, whether you are a piano tuner, a plumber's mate, a deep sea diver or whatever, and let me tell you something. Any creep can be a dead saint, the Vatican Council is calling you to be living saints.' I should have noted that the non-believers and members of other Christian denominations in Nancheng shared the views of the Catholics about Tom.

But how about the priests of the diocese? We priests are much slower to be impressed by the holiness of our fellow priests than are the laity. In the 'Wild West' they were 'quick on the draw'. We priests are rather quick on the flaw, when we are told of the holiness of a fellow priest. I have visited hundreds of presbyteries and never once has a pastor called me aside and warned me that the curate was a walking saint. Reflecting on this, and with an open mind, I approached Pat Dermody, to whom Tom was sent as curate to Nanfeng in 1934. 'Pat', said I, 'what is all this business about the sanctity of Tom Ellis? Do you regard him as a saint?' To my consternation Pat shot back without hesitation. 'There is no doubt about it.' Pat died in 1990 and I asked him about Tom a few years before that. His testimony is all the more valuable because he was fairly 'quick on the flaw', a plain blunt men you could say. And indeed he was outspoken about disagreements he had with Bishop Cleary, although both are in full agreement about Tom Ellis. Pat was not the type who saw the good and nothing but the good in everybody. When I asked him about Bishop Cleary's predecessor, Fr Tierney, he was not even outspoken, but his silence was most eloquent. With his lips tight shut and deep sadness in his eyes, he just shook his head from side to side two or three times. Cornelius Tierney was a man of prayer and mortification and died in the hands of the Communists, while his release was being negotiated in February 1931.

Well, that is the testimony of a man who was Vicar General for over twenty-five years and I think he was expressing the views of all the priests there. Having heard the testimony of the Vicar General, perhaps we could again call on Bishop Cleary. I quote from his letter: 'When I appointed Tom Ellis to Nanfeng in 1934, some of the Catholics there thought Tom mildly mad. They came to this conclusion because of his first day walking down the streets of Nanfeng, he encountered a dysentry patient (dysentry is a type of diarrhoea prevalent in the tropics and it is very debilitating) in a loathsome condition. Tom brought the sick man to the church somehow and scrubbed him clean and was about to wash his clothes when some Catholic proposed to do it. Tom never recovered from that madness though it took him some years before it developed to its full grandeur in Nancheng.' Tom's madness was akin to that of St Camillus de Lellis who died at the beginning of the seventeenth century and to that of St John of God, who died in the middle of the sixteenth century.

In the Divine Office we read about the former: 'The charity of Camillus was so great and wide ranging towards his neighbour and especially towards the sick, the wretched, the dying, that he seemed to burn himself up and wear himself out with the utmost devotion and compassion.' Tom was back in Nancheng in 1938 after a four-year stint in Nanfeng. Bishop Cleary continues: 'His early years were years of hard fruitful pastoral work. On Christmas Eve 1938 he and Fr Dennehy had 133 baptisms and 700 confessions in Nancheng parish, a clear proof they were not letting the grass grow under their feet.'

But despite his arduous pastoral work in Nancheng parish, the 'creeping' madness that Tom contracted in Nanfeng took a more serious turn when he returned to Nancheng, and could be described as a 'galloping' madness. The bishop goes on in his letter:

'He had by that time, i.e. Christmas 1938, begun to collect 'specimens', down and outs whom he set making beads and candles to save them from making idols for a living.' But despite his commitment to the destitute, the outcast, the flotsam and jetsam of life, nobody in the community suspected at that time that Tom was threatening to be a saint. The question I ask myself now is, at what time did the first dark suspicion of his fanatical intentions enter their minds? With hindsight, and I have a remarkable gift of hindsight, I would say when the Japanese army burned the city of Nancheng in June 1942. Even our Catholic Mission hospital did not escape, though all the other buildings in the compound escaped the devastation. The day after we arrived in Nancheng, 4 December 1946, we saw what a savage devastation had taken place in the city.

But what earthly connection did the burning of Nancheng have with Tom's growth in holiness? Some words of Matthew Arnold, English poet and critic, have helped me to see the connection. The words are, and I quote, 'For the creation of a master work of literature, two powers must concur, the power of the man and the power of the moment, and the man is not enough without the moment.' It is with life as it is with literature, it seems to me. The saint is the master work of our human kind. Tom had the potential with the grace of God to achieve that master work in his own life. The devastation of Nancheng in 1942 made the potential an actuality.

After Nancheng city was destroyed, the city was soon filled with refugees from all over the country. As a collector of 'specimens', Tom was soon in the 'big time'. According to Bishop Cleary's letter, Tom might carry a very weak 'specimen' from amongst the refugees on his shoulders and wash him, if there was nobody else available to do so. After the hospital was burned, the bishop set up another little hospital. He tells us about it in his letter: 'We had recently opened our little hospital which was then, and is still, almost exclusively a refuge for the ulcerous, evil-smelling common, tuberculous, enteric, down-and-outs in Nancheng. Here, at the end of a heavy day's work, he would sit at a table, or perhaps on a patient's bed, and talk to the poor creatures as a friend and father, unfolding to them the mystery of God's love for each of them, sending many of them to death with a radiant smile of love and gratitude.'

But as well as bringing spiritual consolation to the dying refugees, he had to try to provide a livelihood for increasing numbers of living refugees. Here the man was equal to the moment. God had given him multi-purpose hands. Listen to Bishop Cleary telling us what Tom could do with his hands: 'Later, as increased accommodation had been given him for his works he had to install an electric plant, perfect a contraption for making beads by re-organising parts of a sewing machine, make moulds for crosses and medals, learn to smelt brass and aluminium, and investigate the mysteries of electro-plating. As well as that, he had to install a printing press of sorts, set it in operation and train his rag-tag and bobtail to use their hands a little more economically. He had to do all this in the heat of a Nancheng summer. It was nerve-wracking, but one suspects he had discovered how to have "workful distractions" at prayer, for otherwise he could not have endured what he must have suffered.'

A saint of the technological age, you could call him. Bishop Cleary tells us that he had seen engineers (American, Australian, or European engineers passing through Nancheng would usually stay at the Catholic Mission) gape in astonishment as Tom discussed engines, wind chargers, charcoal burners, the annealing of metal, the making of shot, the tanning of leather, the latest popular ditties – anything, everything.

Tom was not only a 'Jack of all trades' but he seemed to have mastered many of them. As well as that, he had the ability to teach his refugees (who were not ill) to become semi-skilled at the little industries he had set up to provide them with food and lodging in the compound. He seemed to have employed everybody and to have trusted everybody he employed. Strange to relate, they seemed to prove themselves worthy of his trust, even the jailbirds. On one occasion, according to the bishop, Tom employed a jailbird to prepare bean curd (made from soya bean and it is very nourishing) in the compound. When somebody asked Tom if he thought the man was reliable, Tom replied with a smile, 'He should be, he is the last man out of jail' – presumably he means that the more recently a jailbird has been released, the more likely he will be reliable.

Be that as it may, Bishop Cleary thinks that the guidelines which Tom followed in his dealings with refugees were twofold. The first was 'See Christ in every poor or afflicted man and treat him as the Blessed Virgin would treat him'. The second was 'Do the present act perfectly and God will help at the next'. These inspiring and very practical resolutions were chosen after a much prayerful pondering, and after much trial and failure. But how admirable they were for a priest in Tom's apostolate and how practical.

Some aspects of the teaching of Confucius resemble Christ's teaching, but Confucius has nothing remotely like 'What you do to the least of these my brothers you do to me'. On the contrary he teaches courtesy is not to be extended to the commoner nor punishment meted out to the lord. No wonder the Communists gave the red card to Confucius and sent the Sage and his books to the side line. I understand the present regime in Beijing have, to some extent, rehabilitated Confucius, partly because his name promotes tourism etc. But no follower of Confucius would dream of extending to 'the commoner', the courtesy, the Christlike compassion Tom and his co-workers extended to them.

Tom had many failures in his efforts to put into practice his superhuman resolutions. But after each failure, he started again with God's help, Our Lord rising each time, after the three falls under the cross, never very far from his mind. The example of the 'Little Flower' and Francis de Sales must have helped him too. But God's help was also so generous that, during the last few years, seeing our Lord in each refugee and trusting completely in God seemed to become second nature to him.

CHAPTER 9

A Son among the Saints

Bishop Cleary gives us a picture of Tom's pastoral activity shortly before he contracted the fatal typhoid in February 1945. The Bishop writes: 'During the last few months of his life, he visited his mountain missions in weather which was bitterly cold, and lent his coat and shoes to a carrier, whom he had to send down to the city. He found a dead soldier by the wayside, and turned aside and buried him. When he returned to Nancheng, he went on a round of 'feasts' with the poor refugees in the compound to put some self-respect into them, and showed that he was not too grand to share their poor meals. During a two week fall of snow, he slaved in the hospital with a crush of 80-90 derelicts, who were flung on his hands in appalling conditions, with frost bite, relapsing fever and other diseases. At one time he had seven corpses on hand, because he could get nobody to bury them (they were on ice, he said, perfectly safe). He investigated a primitive de-louser in a neighbourhood camp, and proceeded to erect an improved edition. He flung his last cent, say £5.00 which had come to him as a "windfall" a few days previously, into the hospital to help purchase little extras for the poor sufferers. He met the beggars, that seemed to rise out of nowhere at the Chinese New Year. Patiently, investigating all the cases (it was snowing hard) he helped the genuine ones. He planned a re-organisation of his doctrine school and made arrangements with the parents for the admission of their children.'

Sometimes it was not merely a matter of working with him, it was a matter of slaving with him. When the intake of refugees and derelicts was big, they slaved with him for weeks on end, and while Tom brought the organisational ability and the expertise in the different fields of mechanics, the sisters brought the sympathy, the compassion, the feminine touch, the healing, to people, for whom everything seemed hopeless, in that miserable refugee camp.

The sisters and Tom seemed to have made a superb team. For that reason, it is only natural that he would have confided to the sisters about his fears, his hopes, his depression, his disappointment with the slow progress he seemed to be making in his spiritual life. Later when things seemed to improve on the spiritual front, so to speak, Tom also shared this with the sisters. Sister Baptist was an intelligent person and a woman of wisdom. After she qualified in University College Galway, she lectured briefly in that University, before becoming a Columban Sister. She was a native Irish speaker and had spoken to Pádraig Pearse as a child, when he came to learn Irish in Rosmuc. Tom gave her his notes, although he had lent them previously to Tim Beecher for his retreat – for Tim's last retreat.

Although Bishop Cleary had not seen the notes before Tom's death, Sr Baptist gave them to him some time after the funeral. He abridged them, but did not edit them in the sense of correcting mispellings etc. Tom did not edit them either. In the next chapter, I shall hand you over to Sr Baptist, and she will give us an enlightening and inspiring but rather brief commentary on the notes. Her commentary will be in the form of an introduction, and then I shall share with you some extracts from the notes not already quoted by Bishop Cleary. But right now let us follow Tom's activities as recorded by Bishop Cleary.

> 'To crown all, he personally conducted two missions (retreats) for the people of Nancheng. One for the men and the other for the women, each of three days. The next day he set out for Nanfeng to conduct another mission there in a country mission station for his old pastor, Fr Dermody. He had delivered two days lectures and heard 61 general confessions when he went down with typhoid which he had probably contracted at one of the 'feasts' here in Nancheng.
>
> He had no reserve of energy to fight such an illness and he lasted only a few days. Fr Con O'Connell arrived on the second day and gave him the last sacraments and nursed him for a few days. He suffered a good deal, for he remarked he

did not think that typhoid could be so painful, but he never complained. Dr Otto Homberger, his friend, came from Nanfeng in an effort to save him but he died on the morning of 8 March, the Feast of St John of God, whose vocation he shared.'

Bishop Cleary sums up saying: 'The battle is over and I have no doubt that he is at rest.' Once Tom wrote: 'Suppose that when Our Lord fell on the 3rd, 7th and 9th stations, it was my turn to console him, what could I say or offer? I couldn't say "Keep up now, you have not far to go." But I could offer him something I was thinking of refusing and go to it with increased zeal.' The bishop continues: 'I think he spent his life, especially those last intense years, offering things to console Our Lord and sometimes falling.'

During these last intense years, the years when the madness he caught in Nanfeng back in 1938 had reached its full grandeur, Tom's spirituality seemed to be Christ centred, specifically centred on the suffering Christ. Here is a thought of Tom's: 'To carry the Cross daily. Let everyday be a lifetime. Divide the day into 14 stations, let the meditation be the forseeing of what is to happen.' Another thought from his notes goes like this: 'The Cross cannot be escaped, so with Our Lord in the garden, let us agree to suffer if it be God's will.' These thoughts of Tom's remind me of some words of Pascal, the French writer. He writes: 'Jesus will be in agony until the end of the world. We must not sleep during that time.' Tom did not sleep; he watched during these last few years of mortifications and sacrifices willingly and joyfully accepted. Of course, devotion to our suffering Lord manifesting itself in various types of penances and mortifications, like St Patrick's purgatory or Croagh Patrick, was part of his heritage as a spiritual child of St Patrick. For that reason, I think Tom's mother would have more easily understood the letter which Bishop Cleary sent to her after Tom's death telling of the austerities of his life. The letter went:

Dear Mrs Ellis,

This is not a letter of sympathy; it is a letter of congratulations on having a son among the saints.

The bishop then tells her the event which happened in Nanfeng in 1938 where Tom was seen scrubbing the man stricken with dysentery and wallowing in filth. He assures her he did not hear of the incident till after Tom's death. The letter goes on that 'had I heard of it in 1938 I would have discovered earlier where Tom's true vocation lay.' The bishop continues, and I quote: 'It was years before I finally made the discovery, but thank God I did so in time to enable him to put in half dozen years of heroic self sacrificing labour amongst the destitute and undesirables, the sick and the loathsome of the city.

'Tom barely missed formal martyrdom (his reference to the incident related by Jim Yang where a Japanese bullet missed Tom by inches); instead he died a martyr of charity. St Vincent de Paul, St John of God etc would have hailed him as a brother.'

The bishop continues: 'Fr Tom had always been an exemplary priest but towards the end of 1939 he made a retreat which was to be the turning point of his life. Henceforth his aim was not sanctity, but heroic sanctity. We who worked with him could see him growing spiritually as the years went by till in the end we, one and all, knew we had a saint in our midst. He was hard on himself; calmly, methodically, almost cold bloodedly he thought out his spiritual system (he has left his notes covering the period from 1939-1941) and then went out and lived it in all its thoroughness.

'For him, every poor man was a Christ to be consoled and relieved; if there was no poor; Christ was to be consoled by Tom's own self sacrifice. That was all. But it made him live a life such as not one in thousands could live it: dragging his tired feet through the dusty streets into shacks in search of destitute, victims of war, sitting by fever stricken beds to instruct and console the dying, providing work for men and women, whose only passport to employment was inability to earn a living otherwise, dining with the poor he had succoured to put some respect into them; living all the time under the threat of a perforated intestine, or suffering from the weakening effects of malaria. But, as he said again and again during the last months of his life, his soul was at peace and he was intensely happy.'

The late Mark Kelly was a fellow curate with Tom for some years in Nancheng prior to Tom's death. Mark had this to say: 'During the last three years of his life, a change came over Tom, some kind of a conversion and he was certainly a saint during these last three years. He used to go out to the Cathedral each night after we had our cup of cocoa, and in the winter he would take a storm lantern with him and in the cold church he would pray for two or three hours before the Blessed Sacrament.'

I presume Bishop Cleary had this in mind when he wrote his letter to Mrs Ellis: 'If there were no poor, Christ was to be consoled by Tom's self sacrifice.' Bishop Cleary's letter to Dr O'Dwyer and his letter to Mrs Ellis complement each other. The letter to Mrs Ellis was published in the Australian *Far East* in October 1945.

But how about the people and priests and sisters, who worked with the man they regarded as a saint? It could not have been easy for them when you consider his long hours of prayer, his wearying and distasteful work, the stresses and strains under which he laboured day by day. He must have been an edgy man with a 'very short fuse', one would think. Bishop Cleary, however, informs us that this was not the case: 'Tom proved how wrong was the old definition "A martyr is one who has to live with the saints." His simplicity was charming. "I am as bad now as I was ten years ago," he said one morning to a visiting priest. That night he called the priest aside and said to him, "What I told you this morning is not true, there is some improvement."'

Part of his simplicity was that he was prepared and anxious to talk about the spiritual life with anybody. In those days, that type of simplicity was very unusual; priests talked about the bishop, the pastor, the world situation, about football, a little more about the bishop, and maybe a little more about the pastor. But when I was a young priest I never heard them talk about the spiritual life. It was not the done thing, but charismatic renewal has changed all that.

The priests who lived with him found his openness and simplicity refreshing. The Bishop goes on: 'He disliked mere gossip because of its tendency to veer towards the uncharitable, but he was no wet blanket. If we wanted a song he gave us one; if we wanted ten he gave us ten from his inexhaustible supply. It was all part of an apostolate he exercised quietly amongst the priests. If a song helps to relax taut nerves, then by all means let us have a song. It is often better than a sermon. And to add to the simplicity he talked a lot about his Aunt Maggie.'

Con O'Connell, who gave Tom the last rites and nursed him, and finished the retreat he had started in Nanfeng parish, had this to say in his letter of sympathy to Tom's mother: 'God in his Divine Wisdom has seen fit to take to himself the most prized treasure of this vicariate. That treasure was none other than your son Tom. T.E., as he called himself, was everybody's friend, and we all appreciated his ready wit, his unfailing humour and his glorious resonant voice in song, his untiring zeal. We value most of all the fine example he gave us all of a saintly priestly life.'

Con tells me Tom would play cards if priests in from the missions wanted a quorum to have a game, but not often. He enjoyed a Wild West story as well as the best of them; he would drink a glass of Chinese wine on feasts and other occasions that called for it. On St Patrick's Day and on St Columban's Day, when everybody was singing, he would sing along when asked and he was always on demand. He liked an argument, according to Con, especially about Chinese characters and their different meanings and tones.

Teddy McManus, also wrote a letter to Tom's mother when Tom died. Teddy was bursar and there was very little money around during the Japanese occupation and afterwards, and Tom must have made many demands on Teddy's slender resources. Here is what Teddy has to say: 'We have lost a fellow worker. One whom we will always love and to whom we will look forward to help us in our work. Our society never had and never will have a better missionary. When he was not out instructing and helping the poor and unfortunate, you were sure to find him in front of the Blessed Sacrament.'

Tom was 'quick on the quip' ever since he became a seminarian. The day he entered St Columban's he was exchanging names with another freshman; he said to him, 'The name is Ellis. Remember the hangman.' The current hangman was called Ellis apparently. I was nine years old at the time and am surprised that I never heard of him, but then, I suppose, hangmen, for different reasons, keep low profiles. In Nancheng, the other priests, Chinese and foreign, found Tom 'good crack', a joy to be around.

Bishop Cleary goes on to tell us that, in spite of the 'many irons Toms had in the fire', he did a lot for his fellow priests. The bishop writes: 'Hard on himself, he went to considerable trouble to help other priests. Back in 1940 he got the priests to contribute what they considered their best Chinese sermons, and had them printed and distributed to the other priests to help them in their work. He tried to produce a series of lessons with phonetics and translations, to teach the priests to read the Chinese newspaper more easily.' The Communists, in fairness to them, simplified the Chinese newspaper so that with a knowledge of a thousand Chinese characters, we who had never gone to Chinese school or even met the 'scholars coming home', could read it. Before that, one needed to have a knowledge of four to five thousand Chinese characters to read the newspaper. I quote again from the bishop: 'When foreign newspapers ceased, he issued a bulletin with the latest radio news. He liked to visit priests in lonely places and give them a few days of absence.'

But the question now arises. If Tom did not make martyrs of the people with whom he lived, and we have heard the testimony of three of them, how in the world did he become a saint? Well apparently he ardently desired to become a saint since he did his spiritual year in St Columban's; then he worked hard at it according to the spiritual foundation which was laid down for him in the seminary. He worked as hard in trying to answer God's call to holiness that he kept occasional notes from 1939, starting on 28 April 1939 and finishing on 6 August 1941.

In these notes, Tom is monitoring his spiritual growth, so to speak, reasoning with himself, comparing his resolutions against his performance, since his last retreat, since his seminary training. He reminds himself that he has to adapt his life to the China scene. He has to burn into his consciousness that there are more mortifications laid on in China for the European missionary than the missionary is able to handle. He has to be always bringing home to himself that the mortifications that come your way are the safest and the most salutary. In the notes, he is always increasing his supply of hope from the example of the 'Little Flower'. Tom's notes remind me of a golfer who is trying to improve his game and if possible reach the perfection of Faldo, Ballasteros, Nicklaus. So with this end in view he watches the spiritual masters and then with one eye on the saints, like the 'Little Flower' and St Francis de Sales, he spends a lot of time trying to improve his patience, faith, hope, love and so forth.

So eager was Tom to become a saint, that he typed his spiritual notes. And in the body of the notes, he writes three letters to God. There are three 'Dear God' letters. Now though the letters are about very serious subjects of interest to God and to Tom, I exploded with laughter when I saw them. I thought of a man called Voltaire, who built a church in Switzerland and wanted it dedicated as follows: 'To God from Voltaire.' Voltaire, who died in 1778, was a French writer and philosopher and was quite anticlerical. I should think it is over forty years ago since I read his life, but my association of ideas faculty is rather mischievous and light-hearted and all I remember of the life is what I have quoted.

But the letters from Tom to God were serious and helpful. Bishop Cleary, in the letter he wrote to Dr O'Dwyer, quotes a number of times from Tom's notes.

Tom's heroic work with the refugees would have been impossible without the heroic work of the team of Columban Sisters, who were his co-workers. He was in charge, but the six sisters – Srs Michael Mongey, Baptist Connolly, Frances Monaghan, Monica Finn, Berchmans Dooley, Dolorosa Ryan – looked after the kitchen, the hospital, the different industries that Tom had set up. Day by day, the sisters worked with him in the compound, in the orphanage and in the old people's home, whereas the other priests resident in Nancheng would be at the schools or out at the country mission stations or wherever. The sisters knew more about Tom's work and trials than anybody else.

CHAPTER 10

Soul Scan

Without adverting to it, I now realise I have been promoting the cause of Tom Ellis the saint for the past two chapters. Please do not blame me altogether for this. It all started that December morning in 1946 when Jim Yang switched his role of storyteller about Tom Ellis the hero, to the role of advocate for Tom Ellis the saint. We were the jury to whom Jim presented the case for Tom's holiness in measured and balanced language. We young priests.

The time has now come for me to call the most important witness in the case. She is the late Sr Baptist Connolly. Tom left her his notes, and the bishop had not seen them before Tom's death. We are very grateful to her for preserving this valuable evidence for us. God had endowed her with gifts of intelligence and wisdom.

The way I see it now is this, Tom was 'commander' of a refugee camp during the Japanese occupation, but the sisters were his 'lieutenants'. They supervised the little industries, like spinning and so forth, that he set up, and without their competence and heroically hard work, what Tom accomplished would have been impossible. Nearly all Tom's work was done in the compound amongst the orphans, the sick, the refugees, the hospitalised, the down-and-out, the destitute, and the jailbirds. Seeing that he worked so closely with the team of sisters, it was only natural that he should plan with them, and that he should share his hopes, his fears of losing his mind, his feelings of depression, his failures and his ever-growing desire for holiness, with them.

Sr Baptist had quite a mature judgement and was slow to panic just as she was slow to get over-enthusiastic. I know all this because she was very helpful to me when I was the first Columban to be expelled from my parish by the Communists, and to be tried as a criminal in 1950. She was also very practical, because she always organised our community 'man of prayer', and got him to pray before the Blessed Sacrament during the many times in which I was called down for interrogation to the Commissar's office.

For all these reasons, I can well understand how Tom Ellis would have confided in her. Gerry Ellis, Tom's nephew, who has been a Columban missionary in Korea for over forty years, tells me Tom was confessor or spiritual director to the Columban Sisters in Nancheng at that time. So, it is quite probable that he confided his fears and worries and hopes to some of the other sisters too, but she was the one who was entrusted with his spiritual notes. Gerry Ellis told me that she cut out some of the irrelevant parts. The title of her short introduction to the notes is 'Reference to Notes of Fr Tom Ellis'. The introduction goes as follows:

> You may be disappointed at finding such ordinary things troubling him and nothing really original in his ideas as seen in these notes, but please remember:
>
> a) It was when he was getting over a very trying period, between ill health and lack of understanding on the part of those he was living and working with, that he wrote these. In fact, his opening words give you that. He was wearied out in his efforts to serve and please and no one quite appreciated his hidden and arduous labours.
>
> b) His real growth came after 1940 and, as he told me himself, God put him on the 'heights' in 1942/3. By 1945, he was so advanced in conformity with God's will and so adept at seeing Our Lord in every one and in every call, that notes were outside his work. He couldn't very well have given the time anyhow as he had no time to himself.

The introduction is just signed 'By one who knew him', and beneath it in longhand, Sr M. Baptist (SSC)' and under it 'R.I.P.' Sr Baptist died in 1963 at the age of 62. Some other sister must have written her name on the document after her death.

The document is of great value because Tom himself in the last years told her that God had placed him on the 'heights' and she had seen him in the depths of discouragement. She must have witnessed his ascent from the depths to the heights. What a fascinating story of the ascent she could have given us, and perhaps she would have given us, had she not died at the comparatively early age of 62.

It is more likely, I think, that she would have shied off telling us about him. I must confess I laughed heartily when I saw the notes signed just 'one who knew him'. I was not laughing at Sr Baptist. I was laughing at myself because I had the same mistaken idea about humility. When Seamus O'Reilly and I flew into Seattle from Tokyo after China in February 1953, two editors of American Catholic papers, accompanied by Columban Father Joe McDonnell, were awaiting us. One of them, a priest, said to me, 'I would like to interview you, and to get your experience under the Communists in China.' I excused myself saying that in our training, humility was very much stressed, and that I did not like talking about myself. At this, the editor in that picturesque American slang 'blew his top' and 'bawled me out'. He said, 'Gee, Father, you are the only wire through which the news gets to the people.' How right he was! What a pity Sr Baptist had not met that priest editor. In my capacity as 'the wire through which the news' of Tom Ellis' ascent to holiness 'gets through to the people', I shall now share with you some thoughts on the spiritual notes he left behind.

The first thing to remember is that Tom was 33 years old when he started writing these notes. He was nearly eight years in China, and apparently he felt that keeping spiritual notes would help him to discover how well he was building on the spiritual foundation given to him in the seminary, and how practical he was in his application of that spirituality to the China scene. These spiritual assessments of his progress or failure were made during the six days of his annual retreat, and also at other times during the year. The other times would be when he was holding down the parish for one of the priests who was a long distance from Nancheng. He often did this to allow priests, who were on their own, to come into Nancheng for a rest. Going to China in the early days of our Society, was seen as an exercise in 'carrying the cross'. Our mission poet, Fr Pat O'Connor, uses the words 'To take the cross and go' about those going to the mission.

It took Tom quite a while to see that there are more than enough crosses in China, besides looking for extraordinary ones. Tom in the beginning went looking for mortifications, like deciding to do the more perfect thing when there was a choice, and asking himself if he should not forego his leave of absence to Ireland. Every ten years the early Columbans were due a holiday. During his assessments and during the writing of his notes, he realised that he had made such heroic and unpractical resolutions and broken them as quickly as he made them. So conscious was he of this that he says that his guardian angel must have had a fit of laughter when he saw the making and the breaking of the resolutions.

Typing his spiritual notes also brought home to him very powerfully that whilst he was making and breaking heroic resolutions, he still had quite a bad temper. He describes one of his outbursts of temper thus: 'I went into the juiciest of rages.' Not only did he make the angel guardian laugh at the inconsistencies of the resolutions he made in the first years of his priesthood, but he also laughed at himself. His humour breaks through, when he is telling us how he likes to be thought well of, how he likes his work to be appreciated. 'Like the Mohill corner boys, it is not money we want but respect, 'face'... yet who is honouring me – a few who are just as uncertain of salvation as I am?' Tom was a native of Mohill, Co Leitrim, and was educated at St Mel's College, Longford.

With the help of his typewriter meditations, he began to see that his heroic resolutions covered hypothetical cases in the future. I quote from his notes: 'Just now I am being good in the future, and not worried about the now. So now the slogan is "Do whatever God wants of me now; let the future take care of itself."' Some spiritual writers say that each of us has an angel of darkness corresponding to our guardian angel, to thwart the efforts of the former. Tom felt that his angel of darkness, of whom (like St Patrick) he was very conscious, must also be in stitches laughing when he saw Tom wasting energy in reasoning with himself about what he would do in cases that were purely hypothetical.

Tom did not like to be laughed at, especially by an angel of darkness. So he decided to give up making ever-ever resolutions with a few exceptions. He would still hold on to the ever-ever resolutions that were proposed to him when he did the thirty days retreat of St Ignatius during the spiritual year in St Columban's. The resolutions were: to die rather than commit a mortal sin, to die rather than commit a venial sin, to practise sufficient self-denial to strengthen him to carry out these resolutions. Other austerities and mortifications he would undertake when he had the advice of a wise priest. His typewriter also reminded him that he had 'promises to keep' from his past, from his days in the seminary. He had 'promises to keep' – promises made to God as a priest and as a Columban missionary. Henceforth, his watchword would be 'A promise made is a debt unpaid'.

I wonder did the typewriter ever play such a considerable part in helping a priest to grow in holiness as it did in the case of Tom Ellis? He started making occasional meditations on his typewriter on 28 April 1939. I mean he typed out his meditation and reflected on it carefully. Presumably, he started this exercise in Nancheng, but soon discovered that Nancheng was no place for a saint with a typewriter. People would be calling to see him all the time. Then he got the idea from our patron St Columban. Tom writes that St Columban went to great trouble to get away from the cares and worries of this world. Leaving the little huts and enclosure, on the greater feasts he withdrew and threw off the cares of this world.

I found that bit of information surprising, because I thought a monastery was a place where you would take refuge from the cares of this world. But then, I reflected that St Columban was not only big in contemplation but also in confrontation. Columban was a born confronter and he was no respecter of persons when it came to confrontation. He confronted nobles, royalty, even a Pope, when he felt that God's honour indicated that this should be done. So, I suppose, we should not grudge him a break, a get away from it all.

When another priest in the diocese living on his own needed a break, Tom would probably send him a message like 'Have typewriter, will travel.' On 28 April 1939, Tom typed the following mini-meditation: 'The apostles considered they had a treasure (Our Lord) and there also their heart was. Now it is apparent that my treasure must be somewhere else, for my heart is somewhere else. Very hard to define where it is. To say I love myself with a lot of my heart is not far wrong. There is my heart and there also is my treasure. I fear to go all out and love God with my whole heart, and still if I did this, there is not much I could do. Part of my 'all out' would be to recognise how little I am and to love my poverty.'

Echoes of this theme recur in the notes he kept from 1939 to 1941, but I was surprised to find the treasure theme turn up in the last letter of Tom's we have. Bishop Cleary tells us that in December 1944, when, according to Sr Baptist, Tom was on the 'heights', he writes to a correspondent as follows: 'The Kingdom of heaven is likened to a treasure hidden in a field, which when a man having found, hid it and for joy thereof goeth and selleth all that he had and buyeth the field ... now what is the betting, that I shall give up all these little nice things that make life worth living, to pay for the treasure, or shall I pass the field by and say it is too dear? Many people have passed by the same field, and never knew there was treasure in it. I know but shall I give the price? Pray for me. Unless a man renounceth all that he hath, he cannot be my disciple.' Then he refers to Pádraig Pearse's poem:

> For this I have heard in my heart
> that a man shall scatter not hoard,
> ... shall not bargain or huckster with God. *(The Fool)*

Bishop Cleary's comment is: 'He had by that time paid a large part of the purchase price and in the remaining few months he set himself with a vengeance to raise the remainder.' But be that as it may, Tom wanted to get away from Nancheng periodically to give his inner life, his spiritual life, the life of the soul, a chance. A chance to grow and flourish in a genial climate and atmosphere. A mission fairly distant from Nancheng where he was not known would be the ideal place. So, with that in mind, he left Nancheng in November 1939 to make his six days retreat in Luki, our most northerly mission.

In his letter to Tom's mother, after Tom's death, Bishop Cleary says: 'Towards the end of the year 1939, he made the retreat which was to be the turning point of his life. Hence forth, his aim was not sanctity but heroic sanctity.' In his letter to Dr O'Dwyer, the bishop also mentions that retreat: 'With what relief, then, he must have set out on what was probably the most unconventional retreat ever made, taking his typewriter with him. He started at Kiutu and tramped up the hills to Pakan, Kaopi, and Luki, wishing as he went along that he might take all the lovely stones he saw on the road and build them into a beautiful temple for the Lord, resolving to use to the full, his many opportunities of beautifying his spiritual temple with the little sacrifices he can daily make. He wrote letters to God at his halting places.' 'I don't want to be like the rest of men', he tells God, 'I want to give up all, as you want.' What the bishop forgot to say is that from Nancheng to Luki is a matter of fifty miles or more and a lot of it is uphill. Between Kaopi and Luki, there is a famous mountain called the Yang Lao Feng, a mountain of over 1,000 feet, and then from the top of the mountain you descend to the mission at the end of the north line, Luki.

Tramping fifty miles, climbing a mountain over a 1,000 feet high and finishing up with a six-day retreat looks dangerously like a penitential pilgrimage. Tom's mini effort must have reminded him of St Patrick's mega effort at Croagh Patrick and may have inspired him to undertake that unorthodox pilgrimage *cum* retreat.

From my reading of the notes, and I have read them many times, it seems to me that the greatest grace given to Tom by the Holy Spirit was the grace to see that there was a lack of sincerity in his Mass. In the Mass he offered not only our Lord as priest and victim, but also he offered himself. On page 7 he accuses himself of taking back what he offered on the altar in the morning, during the day. The sentence in which he says this is lacking in clarity. Apparently his meaning is that the morning he was ordained, the ordaining bishop said to him: 'Realise what you do, imitate the Reality you deal with' (when offering the holy sacrifice of the

Mass). When Tom offered the Mass, he is telling God that he is the creature, that he belongs to God, soul, heart, mind and body, that also his time and his talents belong to God, and that every moment of his day is at God's disposal. When a priest asserts all this publicity and ritually, God expects sincerity from him, sincerity in his sacrifice; expects him to live the Mass.

Tom feels he is lacking in sincerity in his sacrifice when he does not get up in time to prepare for Mass in a worthy manner. Tom knows that when he offers Mass, he offers himself with Jesus Christ, priest and victim, and that when he loses his temper with some down-and-out, he is not imitating Jesus our Divine Victim. He feels that he is taking back something that he offered in the morning. With great simplicity and humility, he tells God in one of his letters that he finds getting up in the morning almost impossible. This is understandable when one considers how Tom slaved. He admits to Almighty God that he can get up for a few mornings, if his guardian angel pulls him out of bed, and that it seems easy after that for a time. When one considers that Tom was a tall thin man, one would have thought that pulling him out of bed was a little much for a mere angel, and that an archangel would be better equipped for the job. I am prejudiced, I will admit, but I believe my secondary patron, Michael the Archangel, would have been a very good choice.

Enlightened by the Holy Spirit, Tom decided during his retreat that his resolutions for the future must be practical ones. Resolutions which will help him to carry out the duties of his state with greater fervour, regularity and exactness. Resolutions which will help him to make a better meditation, to say Mass with greater fervour, and to improve the quality of his pastoral work, and his visits to the Blessed Sacrament. No more 'airy fairy' resolutions about choosing the more perfect of two virtuous actions when there was a choice'. In the notes, he resolves to prepare for Mass for half an hour before saying it, and to spend a half an hour in thanksgiving. Later on he decided that, in the forenoon, the Mass he had said that morning would be like some soft background music bringing sweetness and light to his work. Likewise, in the afternoon, he would look forward to the Mass he would say the next morning.

By 1943, he was spending three hours in the presence of Our Lord in the Blessed Sacrament each night. I think, therefore, that we are justified in saying that he had paid for the treasure of great price, namely Jesus Christ in the Eucharist and in the poor and destitute, and also in everybody with whom he came in contact. The days of 'huckstering and bargaining with God' were over. Of course, he had begged the Holy Spirit for humility during his retreat because he knew that he was very weak. He realised that no matter how logical a plan for becoming a saint he had devised, he needed God's grace to put it into practice day by day.

The effect of the breviary in his spiritual life was remarkable. In the notes he tells us that, in the past, whenever he got careless about his spiritual exercises, it was something he read in the breviary that brought him back to fervour. He gives us the most unorthodox reason for making a daily meditation that I have come across. The reason he gives is that we proclaim many times in one day's office that it is our great delight to meditate on the Law of God, and to praise him, and to remember his greatness and that he is our helper. If, writes Tom, after saying all these things while praying the psalms, we do not make a meditation each day, then we would seem to be awful hypocrites. He again quotes, 'A promise made is a debt unpaid.'

He was almost obsessed by the fact that he had promises made and that he had promises to keep. But there were not only promises. There were also oaths. He had taken oaths of chastity and obedience when he was becoming aggregated to the Columban Society, both at his temporary aggregation and at his final aggregation three years later. He had also taken these oaths at his ordination. Like the well known author, ex-nun Monica Baldwin, who wrote *I jumped over the wall*, he realised that he could not keep his oaths unless his soul was 'welded to God in prayer'. She regretted having taken the 'jump' as she tells us in the book. But she deeply regretted that she had not become 'welded to God in prayer'.

You could say that a priest's retreat is a kind of a 'check-up' of his spiritual life. It is kind of a 'soul-scan'. 'X-rays' are taken from different angles and perspectives. We have just seen something of what the 'x-ray' of Tom Ellis the priest showed up. Now we shall have a look at the 'x-ray' on Tom Ellis the Columban missionary.

CHAPTER 11

Columban Missionary

It should be recalled that the St Columban Missionary Society or the Maynooth Mission to China, as it was originally called, was only five years in existence when Tom entered St Columban's. It was a Society of secular priests. It is not, and never was, an order and does not have a Rule as orders do. It did, however, have a spirit, and of course it had Constitutions which are laws about how the Society is governed and so forth. The co-founders' objective was to preach the gospel to the Chinese people and to recruit other priests and young men to help them carry out this work. Inspired by the Holy Spirit, they decided that their first priority must be to answer Our Lord's call to holiness, individually and as a group.

When Tom entered St Columban's, he was taught that personal sanctification was to be his primary aim. He was to achieve this by answering Our Lord's call to holiness, to friendship. Our Lord had said, 'I have not called you servants, I have called you friends.' Growth in his friendship was not only the way to holiness, but it would also be the source of fruitfulness in his apostolate when he went to the missions. Growth in his friendship meant spending time with him before the Blessed Sacrament in personal prayer, in visits, in spiritual reading, in praying the breviary, in the rosary and other exercises as laid down in the seminary time-table. It also included cultivating a deep awareness of the Holy Spirit dwelling in the soul. Abiding with him and in his Holy Spirit as the branch abides in the vine was the idea. In all his ups and downs, as revealed in the notes, Tom always wanted to be a saint, to answer Our Lord's call to holiness.

With great honesty, he admits he has doubts about his motive in wanting to be a saint. In page 29 of the notes he writes: 'Perhaps one would like to be a saint with a big fan mail and enough of crutches over the miracles to keep the home fires burning. So the obvious thing for me to do is to fulfil the will of God for me as I know it today here and now – present circumstances. It is laid down fairly definitely for me in the Constitutions and the Canon Law – Meditation, Mass, Divine Office, visit, rosary, work and study.' As Bishop Cleary has noted in his letter, 'his sense of humour was a great help to Tom' in his efforts to become a saint.

In St Columban's, Tom was also taught that fraternal charity should be the badge by which the Columban brotherhood might be recognised in the home countries and might be seen as their witness to Christ in mission lands. Priests and seminarians were brothers in the sense that they took their recreation together, that when seminarians were doing their examinations, there was no professor supervising them. They were left to their honour to keep the rules of the college, and not to copy, because God was always present and they were very conscious of his presence. This came to be known as the Honour System. Tom was taught to be an honourable gentleman and never to do anything dishonourable, in his dealings with God or with other people.

Fraternal charity has many facets and they went in for fraternal charity in a big way in St Columban's, Dalgan Park, Galway. They went in for every aspect of fraternal charity mentioned in St Paul's famous passage in 1 Corinthians 13:4-7: 'Love is patient and kind, it is never jealous, love is never boastful or conceited, it is never rude or selfish; it does not take offence, and is not resentful. Love takes no pleasure in other people's sins but delights in the truth; it is always ready to excuse, to trust, to hope and to endure whatever comes.' They also went in for the 'little virtues', the ones which ministered to charity as St Francis de Sales has described them. St Francis lists courtesy, politeness, cheerfulness, generosity, good manners, thoughtfulness, consideration for others, anticipating other people's needs. These little virtues are very difficult to practice in the wear and tear of daily living unless one sees Christ in the other members of the brotherhood. In Dalgan, the students were constantly encouraged to pay special attention to the virtue of hospitality by welcoming every visitor to the seminary as if he were Christ himself. In fact they were taught that love of neighbour is best practised by trying to see Christ daily in everybody one meets at home and later in the missions – seeing him in everybody, but especially in the poor and the destitute.

From what you have heard so far, you would be justified in concluding that Tom had practised every aspect of love, fraternal charity, mentioned by St Paul and St Francis de Sales, to a remarkable degree. But you have not heard it all yet. What I am going to add now, I had the good fortune to get from four sisters of St Columban who are still alive in Magheramore, Co Wicklow, and who worked with Tom during the refugee period in Nancheng. Sr Monica Finn has this to say: 'That quality of generosity and kindness which Tom practised as a seminarian remained with him and intensified as his life of prayer grew ever more and more intense. For example, if a priest were lonely or depressed, Tom would be off at the first opportunity to visit him in his station, to console him and give him comfort and help … and all this at whatever discomfort or inconvenience it might entail for himself. That quite simply did not matter. When out on a mission station himself, Tom would always be on the lookout for people in need, especially the sick and infirm. These he would bring to the hospital. On one occasion he carried a sick man back to Nancheng on his back for treatment in hospital.' Sister Monica remembers him as a good mixer, sociable, gregarious and always ready to oblige with a rousing song in any gathering, and to lift everyone's spirits when things were bad.

She felt that his works of charity had purpose and direction built into them, and that he was a very astute and far-seeing man. He was always anxious to help the people help themselves to get projects going that would have potential for growth and, as far as possible, would be self-perpetuating.

However, in some of the little industries he planned there were hitches, as there always are, even in the 'best laid schemes of mice and men'. Tom asked Sr Monica and her group of workers to get a knitting class going for the women and girls. 'After a few weeks tutelage they began in earnest with the trial project, a pullover for Fr Tom! The first effort proved to be decidedly asymmetrical. One sleeve was much too short, the other far too long. Sr M. Dolorosa, who was also in Nancheng during the refugee period, is still with us in Magheramore, and she recalls making a sketch of Tom at the time wearing his "Punk" sweater. Sadly this sketch has not survived. Seemingly Tom himself was unaware that he had been caught by the artist, it was all done so stealthily.

Sr Frances Monaghan, who was also in Nancheng with Fr Tom and is now 94 years of age, retired in Magheramore, has some recollections of the Japanese occupation which started, she says, on 7 May 1942. Her account is substantially the same as the one given to us by Jim Yang but it adds a very interesting detail. She says that when Tom Ellis struck the barrel of the Japanese soldier's rifle with his open hand, and diverted the bullet in an upward direction – as narrated to us by Jim Yang – the soldier in question lost 'face'. To regain some of the 'face' lost, he demanded a ring and a watch from the sisters. Sr Berchmans Dooley, who is still living in Magheramore, gave her ring, and Sr Frances Monaghan parted with her nice watch. This pleased, or at least satisfied, the soldier and the happy situation to which all 'face' losers aspire had been reached, namely, 'face' gained. Sr Frances also told us that the sisters remained in the bishop's house for a whole month while the Japanese soldiers were going on tours of 'inspection' in Nancheng.

St John of the Cross tells us 'we will all be judged on love at eventide'. If he is right, then Tom's judgement will a be most favourable one. But in the seminary Tom was taught that the love we show to the neighbour is the love which the spirit has poured into our hearts. We will be unable to practise this fraternal charity, this love, day by day unless we are conscious of the presence of the Holy Spirit in our souls and unless we keep close to the Eucharistic Christ in our midst. Devotion to Our Lord in the Blessed Sacrament was a very important feature of life in the first Columban seminary, when Tom was a seminarian. Fr John Heneghan, first dean of discipline and also editor of the *Far East*, wrote about this as follows: 'We of Dalgan know that after the grace of God, there shall be no greater help in the years to come than the spirit of this house which draws its warmth and joy from the Eucharistic Christ. He is the centre of our warmth and joy and for him we go wayfaring.'

Devotion to the Blessed Sacrament gave the community the distinctive atmosphere of warmth and joy and when Tom went to the missions he brought it with him. He shared the warmth and joy which he got from the Eucharistic Christ with everybody he met in China – in that spiritually cold, bleak and windswept world where the warmth and joy of Christianity were so little known.

Mark Kelly has told us about how Tom spent three hours each night before the Blessed Sacrament for the last years of his life, and Teddy McManus has told us earlier that when you did not find Tom looking after the sick and the outcast, you found him before the Blessed Sacrament. During his last years, Tom spent half an hour preparing for Mass and a half and hour in thanksgiving.

During his training Tom was also told that loyalty to the superior, the rector, the local bishop and the Pope is included in charity. It also demands generosity which, in the seminary, meant keeping the rules and, on the missions, meant giving time to the Lord in prayer so as to grow in his friendship.

There is one other important aspect of fraternal charity with which I must deal. Let me call it co-responsibility. I remember our co-founder, Fr John Blowick, telling us seminarians a few years after Tom Ellis had gone to China: 'The Society of St Columban belongs to you every bit as much as it belongs to me.' His words developed a sense of maturity and a sense of responsibility in us. We were part of the team and that was a great boost for our morale. He spoke those words nearly forty years before Cardinal Suenens wrote his book, *Co-responsibility in the Church*.

It was not Tom Ellis' job to seek out depressed priests and to visit them and counsel them and bring them consolation. It was not his job to visit a priest in a 'one horse' parish and give him a few days leave of absence. It was not Tom's job to give missions or retreats in Nancheng parish or in Nanfeng parish, but he felt he had a co-responsibility to help his people and fellow priests to answer God's call to holiness.

In these examples I have just given, he was practising the generosity, the co-responsibility about which he had been told in Dalgan. He had also been told to develop a spirit of work, a spirit of prayer and a spirit of poverty. Regarding his spirit of work on the missions, I am surprised that he did not die of overwork long before he reached the age of forty. He was not a robust man and the amount of work he took on seems incredible to me. I have dealt at some length with his spirit of prayer, but I shall return to it later. Regarding his spirit of poverty, the bishop has told us how he threw his last few pounds into getting little treats for his 'specimens' amongst the refugees. He tended to give everything he had to the poor.

I have just listed for you the different elements of the Columban spirit, or Dalgan spirit as it was first known. This spirit was instilled into Tom and his fellow seminarians. Its different elements were held up to them as ideals to which they should aspire, as a blueprint for growth in holiness and as a foundation on which their spiritual lives could be built.

What do the x-rays on Tom Ellis the Columban, taken from different angles and perspectives, show up? They show up positive plus on every aspect of the Columban spirit or charism as far as I can see. But I may be prejudiced and you are the jury. What you have to ask yourselves is this, how did he put into practise the spiritual training given him in the seminary and adapted to the Chinese scene? My guess is that your verdict will be, perhaps, 'admirably'.

Tom joined the Columbans five years after the society started. It was in its first fervour and John Blowick, Johnny Heneghan and Ned McCarthy – and I almost forgot a young man called Patrick Cleary who joined the Society in 1918 – challenged Tom with the high idealism of the charism. Tom responded with generosity in spite of failures due to laziness and irritability. He kept trying so that in the last three years of his life he lived the charism to the full.

St Francis de Sales has written that 'the difference between the gospels and the lives of the saints is the difference between music written and music sung'. These last three years Tom was the living embodiment of the charism. Following from St Francis de Sales, it seems to me that the difference between the charism as preached by John Blowick and lived out by Tom Ellis was the difference 'between music written and music sung'. Tom's life made a sweet haunting melody in the hearts of the Nancheng people. This melody raised their spirits and gave them hope when things were going bad, just as Tom's rousing songs did for the Columban community among whom he lived in Nancheng. It stirred up in them a prayerful devotion to him.

As I have already noted, it was the people who first started to pray to Tom Ellis and who said he was a saint. When Bishop Cleary told Dr O'Dwyer that all the priests in Nancheng and the sisters believed that 'we have a saint of our own' he added the qualification, 'not, of course, anticipating the decision of the Church'.

Tom would have chuckled at the qualification, because he had his own ideas about canonisation. When he read the account of the Little Flower's canonisation and about the ceremonies in Rome, he wrote in his notes: 'Pope, many of the cardinals the greatest in quality, the elite of the world, the biggest show ever put up at St Peter's. All for what? Are people who are prepared to serve God so few that we must make a world fair to celebrate it?' That last sentence says a lot about Tom, about his efforts to become a saint himself, and about his efforts to encourage and help the Chinese Catholics to answer their own call to holiness. What it does not say is that Tom had great devotion to the Little Flower and knew quite a bit of her autobiography by heart.

Of course, Tom was not the first holy man to make facetious remarks about canonisation. Monsignor Ronald Knox in one of his spiritual books writes: 'I will never be canonised. They will find the hair cream.' If they found the hair shirt, he would have had a better chance. I know a Columban who asked our bursar, Ned Lane, a question that went something like this: 'Ned', he said, 'If I go all out to be a saint, will you put up the cash?' Ned took the black cigarette holder out of his mouth with his left hand, and blew a little whiff of smoke and then gently replied, 'Ah, we don't budget for canonisations. Besides, the overheads, I understand, are astronomical. They are out of this world.'

My guess is that Tom would not want to be a canonised saint, but he would want all of us to be uncanonised saints without any fanfare or trumpets. Fr Martindale SJ, in his book *What are saints?*, has a chapter called 'Saints with a small st'. He believed there are many hidden saints. It has been observed that a saint is one who believes that God loves him or her. Tom tells us in his notes that he found it hard to believe this with conviction. Fr Martindale says in *What are saints?*: 'They believe in, act upon, and bank upon with total conviction, things that most of us believe in vaguely. They say that there is only one mistake in life and that is not being a saint.' The Nancheng Catholics and sisters and priests and the bishop believed that Tom Ellis did not make that mistake. But you are the jury and you have a right to reach you own verdict.

I have mentioned that Tom Ellis had great devotion to the Little Flower and imitated her in his efforts to reach what Sr Baptist has called the 'heights'. Another saint who I think helped him is St Francis de Sales. In February 1941, he wrote, 'there is a best possible T. Ellis. God is the only one who knows the design. There is every grade from that down to the pit of hell and I do the designing.' St Francis de Sales, who happens to be my favourite saint, had that idea too, but put it a little differently. He said: 'Each of us has a better self. We should make that better self the norm, the standard up to which we should try to live day by day.' Tom had another thing in common with St Francis de Sales. In his young days, St Francis de Sales was quite bad tempered. When he was bishop of Geneva, Calvinist and Catholic alike said, 'If Francis is so good, what must our Lord be like?' Tom got the better of his temper too with the grace of God. In the last years when someone said to him, 'You are very patient', he replied, 'God knows I have plenty of patience, but I do not know where it came from.'

Bishop Cleary thinks that the patience and peace which Tom

developed during the last few years of his life came to him from the nightmare month in the summer of 1942 when the Japanese took over Nancheng. The bishop goes on, 'He used to admit that he trembled from head to foot, when he heard the tramp of heavy shoes or the thud of rifles on the flagstones, but with the strength which he knew was not his own, he faced what was coming, whether it was a smile, or a 'playful' bayonet thrust. He managed to maintain relations which secured the Community from physical injury. Many times death seemed closer than he wished: there was that day when as he stood between a young girl and dishonour, a bullet whizzed passed his ear and might have given him his martyr's crown; there was that night when the drunken soldier pointed to him with his dagger and shouted 'come along you' and he secured his freedom only after an hour's palaver by Dr Homberger.'

Let me hand over here to Sr Monica of Magheramore, who was present that evening when Dr Homberger followed the Japanese soldier. Dr Homberger said to him, 'Fr Ellis is my friend and if you take him away, you take me too.' Dr Homberger was successful in securing Tom's release because he was a German, and when the Japanese soldier was threatening Tom with the dagger Dr Homberger took out his Iron Cross which he had won as a soldier fighting for Germany in World War I. He reminded the Japanese soldier also that the Germans and Japanese were allies in World War II. He saved Tom's life that night and was such a remarkable character in his own right and such a great friend of Tom's that I must give him a little space here. Not only did he win the Iron Cross for Germany, but he also played soccer for that country. He was a brilliant man with a number of languages and a specialist in his own field.

But how did he get to Nancheng, and how was he mixed up with Tom Ellis? Some years earlier, Tom had been in Shanghai and he needed a doctor for the Nancheng hospital. He met Dr Homberger somewhere or other. Dr Homberger was a specialist in a German city, but a close relative of his reported him to the Nazis, telling them that he had some Jewish blood – which he had. Dr Homberger had to flee the country at once and lost all his property. His valuable stamp album took him as far as

Shanghai and then Providence arranged that Tom and he would meet. Tom offered him the job in Nancheng hospital which he gladly accepted.

Homberger was a Lutheran and an excellent Christian. He was a very good conversationalist and very entertaining and I got to know him when I was based in the seminary. He had left Nancheng at the time and was practising in the provincial capital, Nanchang. Catholicism was new to him, and he was very interesting when he compared the different Catholic missionary outfits which he met.

He told me he was visiting an order, which had missions in China, but were natives of a country in the continent of Europe. He noticed that one of the priests was late for supper, and because of his lack of punctuality he had to go up to the superior and ask for a penance. One day as we were talking, he made a facetious comparison between the Columbans and the order that he had visited. He said, 'The Columbans visit me and they win my money at poker and drink my beer. I visit this other order and the man who is late has to kneel and ask for a penance because of his lack of punctuality!' and then he laughed loudly. Before the Communists came, he joined the Catholic Church and was instructed by Bishop Cleary.

Before I briefed you on Dr Homberger, Bishop Cleary was telling us of the ordeals Tom Ellis suffered during that nightmare month when the Japanese took over Nancheng. Bishop Cleary goes on: 'Yet all the time he had a smile and words of encouragement for everybody. The next nine months were a nightmare in another way for it was a long-drawn out disheartening struggle against sickness, destitution and famine. Money was not arriving from home, and it seemed as if the mission would have to look on helplessly at the hopeless misery which surrounded it. Fortunately, the American Advisory Relief Committee came to our assistance and Fr Ellis, together with the other priests and sisters, flung themselves wholeheartedly into the work. From the Committee's point of view, Tom was merely an executive officer, but to those who watched him dragging his wearied feet in their straw sandals through the devastated city, with an imperturbable patience, sifting out the genuine destitutes, and flooding our emergency wards with half-starved creatures suffering from dysentry, typhoid, tropical ulcers, whatnot, he was a real brother to Vincent de Paul or John of God.'

Bishop Cleary has already told us about Tom's death, so I shall now hand over to Con O'Connell who was with him when he died, who finished the retreat which he had started and who nursed him to the best of his ability. The retreat Tom was giving took place not in Nanfeng city but in an out-mission in Wang-tien-Tang. When Tom took ill after the first two days he thought it was a severe attack of malaria and carried on with the retreat. He was taken to Nanfeng Catholic mission where his friend, Dr Homberger, was then working. Con goes on: 'He left instructions with the catechist to send for me to finish his retreat. I finished the retreat on Sunday morning and, after breakfast, cycled in to Nanfeng to enquire as to Tom's health. The doctor had already diagnosed his sickness as typhoid, and as Fr Dermody was away from home, I became Tom's nurse, and during the four brief days of his illness, did my little best to make his as comfortable as possible.' Shortly after Con's arrival, Tom asked him to give him the Last Rites of the Church. After he had received the Last Rites, he felt better but was in great pain and remarked that he did not realise that typhoid could be so painful. To quote from Con: 'He felt much better after the anointing, and, though he was suffering quite a lot, I heard the rhythmic lilt of a cowboy song on Monday for a few minutes, but as I was very busy at the time I cannot recollect which one it was! It looked as if he were searching for a suitable air to harmonise with is severe pains.

Soon he began to suffer not only from a weak pulse but also from a severe dose of bronchitis. Dr Homberger was there regularly to give him injections and to monitor his sinking condition. Homberger put a tube down Tom's throat in an effort to suck out some of the puss from Tom's bronchial tubes.'

Just as Tom's life was a sweet sounding melody in the heart of the Nancheng Catholics, rousing them to faithful fervour, so it was fitting that on his death-bed shortly before he died Tom should have had the lilt of a cowboy's song on his lips, although he was suffering great pain and exhaustion. The Curé of Ars has noted 'that it is always spring time in the heart that loves God'. For the last few years of his life, it was perpetual spring in the heart of Tom Ellis despite the trials, pains and sufferings, depression, fears, exhaustion and temptations, that he had gone through in previous years.

CHAPTER 12

Watchman for God in Nancheng

Tom Ellis wrote on 22 November 1939: 'The prophets were watchmen in Israel and I am watchman for God in Nancheng.' He was pastor, watchman of the Catholic community in that city. Each member he said, of his flock, was a temple of the Holy Spirit and it was his special job to help to keep these temples clean and holy. Bishop Cleary, writing to Tom's mother, said, 'Tom is gone, but somehow all of us, priests and sisters alike, feel that he is nearer to us than ever.' Earlier in the letter, the bishop has written, 'Fr Tom exercised an apostolate amongst his fellow priests and it may well be that the effects of this apostolate will be more far reaching than even his missionary work.'

Teddy McManus, in his letter to Tom's mother, expresses somewhat similar sentiments. He says, 'We look forward to Tom to help us in our work and in our prayers, now that he has gone to his reward.' What the Catholics said I do not know, but I do know that they venerated him and prayed to God to grant them favours through Tom's intercession. When a little Celtic cross was placed on his grave as a headstone, the Catholics came and knelt at the grave to pray. In August 1952 I began to learn something about the cult of the local people to Tom Ellis.

Just as I had been a part-time pig waiter in captivity, when Mick Moran was pig supremo, so when Mick was expelled, on 3 October 1952, I became his successor as caretaker of the cathedral. You may be inclined to think that there was not much work in looking after the cathedral, and that all I had to do was to open and close it. Unfortunately, there was more than that to it. The Communists demanded that the bishop allow them to use the cathedral for meetings every couple of weeks. At first we all felt that this was impossible, and that we should refuse them. But on mature deliberation, we decided that to allow them to use it for meetings would be the lesser of two evils.

So when they asked for permission to have a meeting, I removed the Blessed Sacrament and after they were finished with their meeting I had to sweep the floor of the cathedral and put the seats back in their places. I say it was the lesser of two evils because if we did not allow them to use the cathedral in this way, they could close it altogether, and we would have no place for Sunday Mass and weekday Mass for the people.

Each year we had a novena in honour of St Columban, whose feast occurs on the 23 November. The novena would start on the 14th and I think the novena started at about five or a quarter past five that year of 1952 and the people came to it in good numbers. On the second or third day of the novena, after Benediction, I cleared away the altar and laid out the vestments for the next day. By the time I had finished this, most of the congregation had left the church. There was always danger, on an occasion such as this, that the Reds would rush in to the church and hold a meeting there or something of that kind. For that reason, after the last straggling old lady left, I walked to the side door and locked it. It was after half past five and already dusk.

Then I continued with my work in the sacristy. When I came out into the church to prepare the altars for the next morning Mass, I looked down towards the baptismal font, and there I saw a priest coming in, a coat thrown loosely over his shoulders. He appeared to be a little stooped. I gave no thought to the matter because Fr John Chang had a key to the church and could open the side door at will. I took it for granted that it was he who was coming in to say his prayers, so I kept on with my work and when six o'clock struck, I rang the Angelus bell, then walked down the aisle towards the side door, and returned to the convent where we were interned.

On my way out, I noticed that the priest, whoever he was, had gone and had locked the door as he left. At supper, I said to John Chang 'you locked the door as you left the church just before

Angelus time?' 'I was not in the Church after Benediction,' he answered, 'I could not have locked it.' 'You mean to tell me you did not come into the church shortly after half five?' 'I certainly did not,' he said, 'in fact I was talking to one of the parishioners outside the church at that particular time.'

Then I asked the bishop, Jim Yang and Seamus O'Reilly if they had entered the Church. None of them had. So after supper we decided to go over to the church and search it to make sure that all the other doors were locked. Joseph Peng, who later died under torture, and Tommy Yu, who did thirty years in jail, were seminarians and they accompanied me. We had flashlamps but could find nobody. The other doors were not only locked, but also barred.

The seminarians were very excited about the matter and we went over to talk to the bishop about it. The bishop paused for a while, and in a mannerism we had come to expect, he looked up towards the ceiling, thought for a minute, and then spoke. 'You know,' he said, 'that probably was no living priest; it may have been someone who has come back. So tomorrow night at the same time would you kindly wait in the place where you saw that figure tonight, and ask him in the name of God if there is anything we can do for him?'

We began to speculate as to who the priest might be; someone mentioned that it might be Tom Ellis. Tom Ellis was buried in the cemetery just behind the church. Recently the Reds had been overturning the tombstone on his grave to discourage Catholics from going there to pray. Every time they knocked down the headstone, I raised it up again and put it into its proper position. Of course we reasoned it might be someone like Fr Tamet, the French Vincentian who had built the cathedral. As Drake, according to tradition, comes back and sounds his drum whenever England is in danger, perhaps one of these dead priests who had laboured so zealously in Nancheng, and who now realised that the church was in great danger, was coming back to warn us in our hour of peril.

The next night I waited, having prepared a few questions in

Chinese, English and Latin. Latin I would use in case it happened to be a French man, because my French accent was so atrocious that I would not even try it out on a ghost. I waited and waited, but nobody turned up. I made allowances for the fact that the ghost might have been held up in traffic, but at last gave up hope.

When I got back to the house where we were interned, they were waiting anxiously to hear my report. They were disappointed that the ghost did not turn up. Nevertheless, I think we all felt pretty sure that somebody had visited the church the night before, and that it was not a living person. Gradually, we all came to the conclusion that it must have been Tom Ellis.

But what was the message? What was his point in appearing in the church? Tom regarded himself as the watchman for the Catholics of Nancheng. In his notes of 14 November 1939, he quotes approvingly the prophet Ezekiel when the latter castigates the shepherds of Israel. One of the things he castigates them for is that they saw the wolf coming and did not warn the flock.

I feel in my heart that it was Tom Ellis and I know that his appearance was a warning. Not a warning that the wolf was coming, because the wolf had already been with us for a few years. A warning that the end was nigh for Nancheng cathedral, the only church in the diocese still left open. A warning too that the institutional Church in Nancheng diocese had been destroyed by the Communists. As McLuhan, the Canadian communication expert would put it, 'the medium was the message', Tom's appearance was the message, and within a month almost to the day of the message being delivered, the bishop had been tried on 14 December and expelled from the country. A month later on 15 January Seamus and I left Nancheng under escort.

On 8 February 1952, when the bishop and all the Chinese priests and McCormack and Seamus and I were tried publicly and marched through the streets and spat upon and beaten and kicked and mocked, the Communists concluded that the Church died that day. The non-believers would have come to the same conclusion. They would have reasoned that no institution could survive the colossal amount of 'face' we lost on that day. When the bishop was expelled, they felt that the Church was buried. For that reason, Tom's appearance was a great boost to the Catholics giving them fresh hope. The melody which his life had stirred up in their hearts lingered on and strengthened their faith and sent them in ever larger numbers to his grave to pray.

I must say I was disappointed when Tom Ellis did not turn up, and that I did not have a chance of having a few words with him. Years later, when we were both living in Navan, Bishop Cleary said to me more than once, 'I should have gone down with you that night, the night we were expecting Tom Ellis to turn up.' Maybe behind his feelings of regret was the conviction that it was indeed Tom Ellis and that, as Bishop Cleary wrote years earlier: 'If I see things aright, this priestly apostolate of his is only at its beginning.' That letter was written on 10 April 1945. In the same letter he also writes 'that we have a saint of our very own watching over us and with us, screaming for help in our need and encouraging us in the fight if we would but look'. In the eighteen years Bishop Cleary lived after leaving China, he must have read that letter time and again, and felt convinced that Tom was helping our Chinese priests and encouraging them in their hour of need. Bishop Cleary was dead about ten years when we received that 26-page letter from Jim Yang, bearing great tidings of heroic witness given by our Chinese priests during the persecution. Even while the bishop was alive, we got little bits and scraps of news through Hong Kong and they were all to the effect that none of our priests had joined the Patriotic Church and that they were all witnessing in jail or in labour camps.

The Little Flower, to whom Tom had such great devotion, said she would spend her heaven doing good on earth. I think God alone knows how much Tom Ellis, the 'Watchman of Nancheng' as he called himself, helped, encouraged, animated, inspired our Chinese priests during their long years in jail, and ourselves too while we were in China. Not only the bishop but Con O'Connell and Teddy McManus also expected that Tom would keep helping us after his death, as they tell us in the letters they wrote to his mother. But what about the Nancheng Catholics whose pastor he had been? We had little news of them during the fifteen years the bishop lived. However, from time to time, we did hear that they were going to Tom Ellis' grave all the time and praying there. This infuriated the Communities to such an extent that during the night they dug up Tom's bones and buried them in different parts of the grounds surrounding the cemetery.

We often said when we were in China that you could not hide anything from the Chinese; they are such a shrewd race – particularly the southern Chinese. And soon our Nancheng Catholics, who were southern Chinese, found the bones that had been dug up and buried them in a place known only to themselves. They guarded the bones as relics. Some of the Catholics kept relics, bits of Tom's bones in their homes. The next thing the Communists did was to decide to build houses in the field which was our Catholic cemetery and in the field next to it also. This would mean that they would be digging foundations for houses and that any of Tom Ellis' relics they came across, they would take with them or destroy. At least that is how the Nancheng Catholics felt about the situation.

As some of our missionaries were passing through Hong Kong, they heard about Tom's bones and when they came back here on vacation, would ask me about Tom. All I could say to them was, 'Well, of course, I never knew Tom Ellis while he was alive. Actually, I never ran across him till he was six and a half years dead.' Some of them regarded that as an 'Irish Bull', but if it was, so be it. The 'Irish bull' is my favourite breed of livestock. I suppose, too, there is a certain amount of snob value in running across a ghost who is regarded as a saint.

Then to my great surprise, I had a letter from Fr Tommy Yu, written on 6 February 1990. In that letter, the following occurs: 'The relics of Fr Ellis, (most of the skeleton) are in a certain place in a white big thick paper box. Would you please tell his (Tom's) nephew to come – to get it back to Ireland. It is unlawful to keep a foreigner's bones in the house. Fr Kelly told me that his nephew wants the relics.' Fr Kelly, an expert on matters Chinese, was our man in Hong Kong. So keen were the Nancheng Catholics on guarding Tom's Ellis' relics that they took them away to a place nearly five hundred miles from Nancheng. The nephew in question was Fr Gerry Ellis, a Columban, who had been a missionary in Korea for nearly forty years. I was rather surprised that Tommy asked me to look after the matter because Fr Kelly was in Hong Kong. Nevertheless, I wrote to Gerry Ellis in Korea and told him about the letter I had received from Tommy Yu.

In his reply Gerry Ellis told me that the Ellis family had expressed no such wish. They felt that as the people of Nancheng revered Tom's bones as relics, then the relics belonged to them. He was of the opinion that the misunderstanding may have arisen in this way. Gerry's sister and her husband were passing through Hong Kong on their way to New Zealand. They enquired if it would be possible to go into Nancheng and to see Tom's grave. They were told that it would not be possible, as things were in China at that particular time.

At the moment of writing, I know where exactly Tom's bones are buried. But I feel pretty sure that when freedom breaks out in China again, the bones, or some of them, will be gathered together and be again buried in consecrated ground in Nancheng. If the little Celtic cross which I so often lifted up and put into position is not lost, it will be placed as a headstone at the head of the grave. If it is lost, the Catholics and the priests, Chinese and Columban, will have another one made. Tom's grave would be a kind of a shrine to which the Catholics will come and pray as they did before the persecution and during it. Hopefully, they will keep up the custom after Communism has completely disappeared in China.

As I have already noted, Tom regarded himself during life as the watchman, the shepherd, of the Nancheng Catholics. Please God he will keep on that role. In his notes of 14 November 1939, he refers to Almighty God's displeasure at the shepherds of Israel because they were failing to do their duty. Almighty God said he would become the shepherd of Israel and I quote the way he said he would do it: 'I will seek the lost, I will bring back the strayed, I will bind up the crippled, and the fat and healthy I will lead forth again' (Book of Ezekiel).

A number of Catholics joined the Patriotic Church through the pressures inflicted on them during the persecution. Some have been lost or strayed or wounded. All need healing, and I venture to hope that Tom's prayers will help to bring about that healing, that reconciliation and forgiveness which will be called for, in the post-Communist era, in Nancheng city and diocese.

For the priests who will be engaged in the apostolate in Nancheng diocese in the years to come, Tom's life will be an inspiration and an example in the fields of work and of prayer. Bishop Cleary has already told us about the mighty work Tom did during his years in Nancheng. Now I shall share with you some words from Bishop Cleary on Tom's prayer life. 'I think his formal prayer to the end was simply a devotional consideration of the Divine Office, and the only 'lights' he got were such as were derived from a more thorough assimilation of the wisdom contained in its psalms and lessons. The breviary had become his *Vade Mecum* (the book he carried around with him) and in his latter days he feared to read any merely ephemeral productions lest they prove a distraction to his recollection. He was a very remarkable illustration of the power of the Divine Office to sanctify the life of a missionary.'

Well that is a very practical aspect of his spirituality and should be helpful to many priests. I have heard and read that quite a few priests are giving up saying the Office right now, not realising its power to sanctify them and make their apostolate fruitful. As I have said, Tom was the embodiment, as far as I am concerned anyhow, of the Columban charism or spirit. He was the kind of Columban that many of us would like to be, but somehow have never managed to become.

Frank Sheed, in his book *The Irish Way*, wrote: 'Every nation has its own way of being Catholic. The Irish way is St Patrick's way.' In his efforts at becoming an heroic Catholic, I think we can say that Tom took after St Patrick, whose spiritual child he was, in a number of ways. He had this nobility of soul which kept urging him on to desire and to strive for heroic sanctity despite many setbacks. As I have noted, he wrote, 'I do not want to be like the rest of men.' The rest of us are more sensible and more prudent and settle for much less than Tom did. St Patrick had this quality to a much greater degree, I presume, as Noel Dermot O'Donoghue tells us in his book on St Patrick, *Aristocracy of the soul*. That title sums up St Patrick's mystical spirituality. St Patrick had a 'laborious episcopate' and from what we have been seeing, Tom Ellis today would be described as a 'workaholic', only that he was a 'workaholic' who seemed to have time for everybody, and who seemed to be a joy around the place, and to have a knack for putting other people before himself. They were both men of simplicity.

Tom mentions twice his angel of darkness and St Patrick was very conscious of evil and of the angel of darkness in his life. They both shared a great devotion to the psalms, and St Patrick would say the 150 psalms of a night. Tom writes, on 14 November 1939, 'Every day we read the breviary and every line has a meaning that could convert our hearts and we should be healed.' Tom could spend quite a long time preparing for the Office he was about to say, trying better to understand the psalms and the readings. In fact, Tom had started to learn Hebrew so that he would not miss any of the spiritual treasures contained in the psalms.

Tom also took after his spiritual father in that he lead an ascetic life, that is according to twentieth-century standards. We of the twentieth century are soft compared with the people of St Patrick's day. The asceticism of St Patrick frightens us, but Tom's resolution to give up smoking and his failure to carry it out, his resolution to get up at a certain time and his failure at that too, all these things give us courage to try to answer God's call to holiness. After all his failures, Tom kept on trying. In his notes of August 1941, he writes words of encouragement 'failing never does matter. Failing to try again is the failure that is without hope'. On 24 March 1940, he writes, 'that according to St Francis de Sales, God has a very special plan for each soul. We find that plan is our state of life and God gives us special graces to become saints in that state.' Tom found that his temperament made him shy of giving the impression that he wanted to be a saint. For that reason, in his notes of February, 1940 he writes '... Quit pretending ... the only proper Tom Ellis is the one God wants me to be. To be ashamed of being myself is surely a false shame. People expect priests to be holy, and we are not ashamed to play at not being holy.' He was so keen that he should become a saint himself and that he should help his people in Nancheng to become saints, that I think the last word he would like to leave us is the quotation from the American pastor which was given in a sermon after Vatican II and which I shall now repeat: 'Vatican II, the second Vatican Council, is calling all you people to be saints. The Council is calling you to be a living saint; any creep can be a dead saint.'

PART II

The Witness of the Chinese People

CHAPTER 13

Pardon and Peace

What about ordinary Chinese Catholics who got caught up in the revolution and involved in the persecution? Up to now, I have only been telling you about heroic people. It is much easier for us ordinary Catholics to admire them than to imitate them. What about some ordinary Catholic whom we can imitate?

That is fair comment and I am glad you have made it. So I shall now proceed to tell you about an ordinary run-of-the-mill Catholic and I hope you will not mind if I tell it in my own way. I trust you will find much to imitate in it and that it will impress you as much as it impressed me.

It was a bright May morning and the tropical sun was beating down mercilessly on the military compound in Red China where six of us Columbans were held in captivity. Manual work had been assigned to each of us. I was a part-time pig waiter. It was promotion for me to get the job and I am afraid I intrigued to get it. It was the only time that I have sought preferment in the Church by intrigue. The pig supremo, Mick Moran, was a friend of mine, and I asked him if he would take me on now and again as a casual pig waiter, and he did so willingly. I carried and served three meals daily to the bunch of black pigs detailed to me by Mick, an older man who had more theology and more missionary experience than I had. Besides, he was something of an expert on the Chinese pig in sickness no less than in health.

The job was not too bad apart from the midday meal. Like the 'mad dogs and Englishmen' in Noel Coward's humorous song on the Orient, we pig waiters went out in the midday sun carrying buckets of swill or mash. At that time of the day, there was a danger of getting sunstroke or heatstroke; in fact, one of our missionaries in the diocese, Jerry Buttimer, had died of heatstroke a few years earlier and we were very conscious of the danger. At the morning meal, however, there was no such danger because the sun was not yet really up. That is why on many mornings, I experienced not only job satisfaction but I fear a little vanity too, as I noted how my far-from-perfect Chinese pig-call roused my pig patrons from their slumbers in the sun and brought them galloping to the trough.

This particular morning the sweat was rolling off me as I returned after serving breakfast to the pigs. I was going inside to wash when I noticed a door opening diagonally across from me on the other side of the compound. Through the open door, a Chinese prisoner clad in prison garb, and carrying a large log of wood on his shoulder, entered the compound. I took my hand off the door knob and watched. To my great surprise, five other Chinese prisoners, heavily burdened by the logs they were carrying, followed the first prisoner into the compound. They looked weary and downcast, and behind them came two armed soldiers, urging them on. As they were coming up opposite where I stood, about forty yards from me, suddenly one of the prisoners lifted his head, looked across at me and raised his free hand as if he were signalling to me. But, I reasoned, a Chinese prisoner could not be signalling to a foreign 'criminal'. Nothing could justify the risk involved, I concluded. My conclusion was wrong because there he was again waving to me, and trying to look in my direction in what seemed a very imploring manner. This time I stared hard at him and to my amazement recognised him. Who should he turn out to be but Yu San Yung, an ordinary Catholic from the parish of which I had been pastor and from which I had been expelled the previous year.

Well I was overjoyed at recognising my parishioner, fellow prisoner and friend and in a flash knew what he wanted. He desperately wanted that blessed sacrament of reconciliation and pardon and peace and healing. So I waved back to him to let him know I recognised him. Then I made a little sign of the cross with my finger to indicate that I knew what he wanted. Immediately he stopped and made his act of contrition slowly and meaningfully with his head bowed. I recited the words of absolution. When I had finished them, Yu San Yung lifted his head, smiled and bowed to me. He seemed to walk on with a lighter step after he received absolution. He looked more peaceful as far as I could see at that distance and seemed a new man.

Though he was still heavily burdened with the log of wood, the much heavier burden of sin and guilt feelings had been lifted from his soul. Yu San Yung and his fellow prisoners were heading for the yard where the firing squad operated and from where we heard frequently the rat-tat-tat of the rifles. I feared he was on his way to his execution. I have since learned he was indeed executed. His fearless faith would have brought him through any eventuality. He was a good man, an ordinary Catholic, and nothing outstanding about him except that his faith ran deep. His only crime was that he had been a member of the defeated Nationalist Party. But that was enough. The victorious leader of the Communist Party, Mao Tse Tung, declared that the Nationalists were traitors and should be exterminated.

I celebrated the sacrament of reconciliation with Yu San Yung in an abridged form, as the circumstances permitted. Yet never has the celebration of this sacrament affected me so profoundly. Maybe it was because I said the words of absolution, not in a whisper as I usually did in the confessional, but in a conversational tone and very deliberately. What I heard myself say in Latin, jolted me. The English is, 'Our Lord Jesus Christ absolves you and I, by his authority, absolve you from your sins.' It was the words 'Our Lord Jesus Christ absolves you' that startled me. I knew, of course, that it is through Our Lord's authority that sins are forgiven, but I had lost sight of the fact that Our Lord is present and active in the sacrament and brings pardon and peace and reconciliation. Some memorable and relevant words from Cardinal Newman come to mind: 'Christ's priests have no priesthood but his. They are his organs and outward signs. When they bless, he is blessing and when they absolve, he is absolving.' Yu San Yung had a meeting, an encounter, with the Saviour who forgave him that day as really and truly as he forgave Mary Magdalen and Zacchaeus, the little tax collector, when they met him.

In that miserable compound on that May morning, with the tropical sun beating down on us without mercy, Our Lord's presence and power in the sacrament of reconciliation were brought home to me most forcefully. The Yu San Yung incident taught me that in the sacrament of reconciliation, there is a Person first, and a process (contrition, confession, satisfaction etc.) afterwards. In the past, as far as I was concerned, the process had tended to obscure the Person.

So profoundly did the Yu San Yung incident affect me that it changed my whole attitude towards hearing confessions. From then on, I welcomed the penitent to the beautiful sacrament of reconciliation where I assured them they were going to meet Jesus, Our Saviour, as really and truly as Zacchaeus or Mary Magdalen met him. These two people in the gospel were never the same after their meeting with Jesus but, of course, their meeting was a meeting by sight. A meeting with him in the sacrament is a meeting by faith but it is the same Jesus, 'yesterday, today and forever', and he can change us as he changed them if we approach the sacrament with sufficient faith and fervour. I did not, by any means, downgrade the process, but I made sure that I put the Person first. I do hope the Yu San Yung story will help you too in this day and age when it is said fewer people are availing of the sacrament of reconciliation and those who do avail of it are going less frequently than in former years.

It is said that we have lost our sense of sin and, if we have, Yu San Yung's example can be imitated by all. So keen was Yu San Yung's sense of sin that he took the serious risk of communicating with a foreign 'criminal' like me in order to be forgiven. So strong was his faith that he even held up a Communist procession of prisoners while saying his act of contrition. As we know, the People's Army of Liberation were capable of punishing very severely any form of insubordination. Publicly practising superstition in co-operation with a 'criminal' who had sabotaged the revolution would add to the seriousness of his crime. Yet to Yu San Yung any punishment they could mete out to him he regarded as trivial compared with the privilege of meeting our Saviour in the sacrament of reconciliation.

There we were that May morning, Yu San Yung and I, two Catholics from opposite ends of the planet, ignoring the Communist soldiers and functioning briefly (each of us with his own particular role) in a sacramental and supernatural world, the existence of which the Communists vehemently denied. The soldiers must have been furious and for a time I feared they would charge me with sabotaging their ideology publicly and in collaboration with a criminal. To my surprise, they did not prefer any charge against me. They had already charged me with sabotage on four counts and perhaps that was sufficient.

The Yu San Yung incident was not the only spiritual 'spin off' that came to us during the three months in which we did manual labour during that tropical summer in 1951. We decided to do the manual labour in order to keep the old people and the orphans alive, and also so that the Communists would not have any excuse for charging us with neglecting them. Despite the danger of sunstroke, that three months was a very joyful period for us and joy is of one of the gifts of the Holy Spirit. After sundown it was amazing how our spirits shot up and indeed I remember one such evening when we felt compelled to write a parody on John McCormack's lovely 'Bird Songs at Eventide', adapting it to the situation in which we found ourselves. All that I can now remember of our effort at parody is 'Pig Songs at Eventide', 'Calling, Calling'. Fortunately for posterity the rest is lost. Taking supper to our pig patrons was the easiest and most pleasant part of the job. Bishop Cleary would sometimes stand at the door of the house, his brush in his hand – his job was sweeping the floors – laughing heartily at the spectacle of Mick and me sallying forth in the cool of the evening, chanting the Chinese pig-call 'con brio' as we went.

The evening meal was the most enjoyable part of our day, as all of us seminarians and priests met together after the deadly sun had gone down. To have survived another day doing manual work under the tropical sun brought a great sense of happiness and well-being to all of us. That there was more joy than meal is no reflection on the culinary expertise of Seamus O'Reilly and Tom Fisher. I suppose you could say that not on rice alone doth man live, though we made a jolly good attempt to do so during these months. After the evening meal, we did the washing up together and the crack was particularly good at this time. Again, I would say there was more crack than 'wash up' because all we had to wash was spoons and chopsticks and rice bowls and cups and saucers and maybe something else.

If, as an English journalist visiting Dublin observed, there is a dramatist inside each Irishman waiting to get out, then I can testify that the dramatist inside Mick Moran generally came out towards the end of the washing up. The drama that emerged was a one act play with two characters. Without any preamble, Mick would suddenly decide to play the part of a Communist official denouncing a landlord, during land division. By aiming his denunciations at me, he indicated that I was to play the part of the landlord in the drama (just as I had been a landlord in real life before my expulsion). Mick knew the Communist jargon and gestures of denunciation as he had been denounced a few times. After Mick's tirade, I was expected to respond as Chinese landlords responded in similar situations. Sometimes I would deny the charge out of hand, sometimes I would cringe with fear and confess my crimes. I would confess that I had indeed fleeced the poor farmers and the workers, but since Chairman Mao had liberated us, my eyes had been opened. I had seen the light.

On occasion we swapped parts, but whoever was playing the part of the Communist official had to raise his voice and shout at the landlord. One evening as Mick and I were doing our variations of the one act drama, after the other priests had left the wash-up room, a Chinese priest happened to be walking in the corridor outside. The priest was John Chang, and he was a sickly man. He heard Chinese voices raised in anger. He stopped. He listened intently. He was convinced that a Communist official was actually denouncing a real landlord, or one of the priests. He got frightened and his face was ashen pale when the drama ended and he looked into the room. When he saw Mick Moran and me, he chuckled with laughter. All the same, we apologised after we explained to him what we were doing. From that time on, we did not raise our voices and our drama lost some of its realism. Public relations, however, were more important to us than realism in our drama.

Looking back now from the vantage point of 1995, we can see that those three months of hard labour in the tropical sun won for us, and for the diocese, blessings that we never could have hoped for or imagined. Not only did they bring peace and pardon to Yu San Yung and a new found joy to us, but they enabled us to have four extra Chinese priests in Nancheng diocese after our departure.

How did this come about? Well, we had no money and the Communists confiscated any money sent to us. We had rice, so we decided to do the manual work and keep the orphans and the old people alive. We hoped that by doing this, the Communists would not expel us. We also new vaguely that we wanted to buy time, but did not know what use we could make of the time or how much time would be given to us.

But the Holy Spirit knew and he had a plan for us. Our Lady, St Columban, and Tom Ellis had parts to play in implementing that plan. A year after we did the hard labour, the bishop was able to ordain our senior seminarian, Joseph Peng, to the priesthood on 6 August 1952. We continued to teach the three remaining seminarians, to the best of our ability. Then Tom Ellis appeared in the cathedral of Our Lady of the Holy Rosary in Nancheng during the novena to St Columban.

On St Columban's Day, 23 November 1952, at tiffin (lunch) one of the seminarians asked the bishop, out of the blue, 'Monsignor, do you think is there any possibility of getting us seminarians into the seminary in Shanghai?' We did not think there was a hope, but the bishop wrote to Columban, Ted MacElroy, in Shanghai. On 8 December, Our Lady's feast day, back came the totally unexpected reply that our seminarians were accepted in Shanghai seminary.

Just six days later, the bishop was expelled. He had the consolation of knowing his seminarians would be priests in a few years. They were ordained in 1957. With forty years hindsight, I am now in a position to share with you what Tom Ellis was conveying to us by his appearance in November 1952. His full message was: 'For you Columbans the end is nigh in Nancheng. Pass your flaming torches to the three young seminarians. They will hold the torches aloft till the persecution has passed.' God's watchman for Nancheng was efficient. His timing was perfect.

But there was one other spiritual 'spin-off' from that three months hard labour as far as I was concerned – you cannot be a part-time pig waiter even for a short time without thinking about St Patrick during his six year stint as a swine herd on Slemish. I am sure Mick Moran, the head pig waiter must have thought often about St Patrick, the swine herd, and must have prayed to him too during that dangerously hot summer.

CHAPTER 14

Prayer Power

Lord Tennyson, the great English poet, made this profoundly truthful statement: 'More things are wrought by prayer than this world dreams of.' We Columban missionaries in Nancheng were at times conscious of, and could almost feel, the power of prayer sustaining, supporting us, giving us courage and hope and joy. Prayers of our co-missionaries in USA, Australia, New Zealand, Scotland, Wales, England, Ireland, raised us up 'borne on eagle's wings', so to speak, above the terror and tension of the cruel Communist regime under which we lived in Red China.

What their good prayers did for us they continued to do after we had left. The prayers of our co-missionaries played a big part in bringing support and comfort and light to 'John McCormack', Jim Yang, and the others years after we had left China. The prayers of our co-missionaries played a big part too, I am sure, in helping Tom Ellis to achieve the degree of sanctity which his fellow priests and the people in Nancheng believed he achieved.

But one example from my own personal experience can give you a better idea of the prayer power of our people, than any amount of talk on the subject in general terms. I received a letter from Sr Teresita Yu, a Columban sister working in Hong Kong, in February 1984. She had a brother a priest in Nancheng diocese, Tommy Yu, who is still alive, thank God. He did almost thirty years in jail. The letter, however, was not about her brother but about Fr Jim Yang, the Vicar General of our diocese with whom I have dealt earlier. Her letter went:

> Fr Jim is dying of cancer in Nancheng hospital, to which he has been transferred from jail. No-one is allowed to visit him or to take him anything. Herbal treatment is all they give him

in hospital. It is terrible. Pray for him and for all our other priests and people.

I can assure you that letter upset me very much indeed. Although I was 10,000 miles away from Jim and had not seen him for thirty-one years, I felt desperately the need to do something for him. I was still a priest of Nancheng diocese, and my fellow priests and my fellow Christians were being persecuted. But why should I be so upset about what seems to be the impending death of one priest? Have I not said in the last chapter that we had four other priests as well as Jim in the diocese then?

Specifically my big worry was that Jim would die before he met Tommy Yu who was next in the chain of command. I felt that the transition was very important, and that it was very necessary that Jim should meet Tommy and brief him and share with him his vast experience. He was about fifteen years older than Tommy and Bishop Cleary had given him a first-class education. Besides, he was regarded by the Communists as the outstanding priest in Jiangxi province.

But how was I going to bring this meeting about? It seemed impossible because Tommy Yu was in jail at this time and I had no idea when he would be released. Even if he were released, there was no guarantee that they would allow him to see Jim Yang. Then it struck me that prayer can do the impossible. It struck me too that very many of our co-missionaries around the world are very near and very dear to Almighty God.

So I put my 'best foot forward', I think it was the left, and sent an article to *The Irish Press* asking for prayers for Jim in particular, and for the priests and people in Nancheng. Well, of course, if you write a straight appeal for prayers to a daily newspaper they will most likely put you in the small ads or articles wanted section, so I decided to write a St Patrick's Day article, in fact to write the story of the 1948 St Patrick's Day match, which I have described in chapter 1. For strategic reasons, I decided to give them the story of the St Patrick's Day match first and just put the appeal for prayers at the end of it. The year was 1984.

We owe a very bid debt of gratitude to *The Irish Press* for their kindness in printing the article and for their great generosity in giving me nearly a page. After quoting from Sr Teresita's letter asking for prayers for Jim, I then quoted from an earlier letter which Jim himself wrote to us in 1980. In that letter, Jim had said, 'we depend on your fervent prayers'.

Then I went on to say that 'these Chinese Catholics belong to St Patrick's spiritual family because we, in collaboration with you, our co-missionaries, have brought the good news to many of them. They depend on us to pray that God will give to all of them, priests and people alike, including those forced into the Patriotic Church, the victory that overcomes the world, "an unfaltering and persevering faith". They depend on us to beg the Lord of history and of time to hasten the day when freedom of religion will return to mainland China and when the feast of St Patrick will again be celebrated in that very happy diocese of ours, with the same Christian joy and lightheartedness as in bygone years.'

The Scottish Catholic Observer, the Australian *Far East*, which is read in Australia and New Zealand, and I believe *Columban Mission*, which is our magazine in America, also carried the article, and so people around the world were praying that Jim and Tommy would be able to meet.

Against all human odds, Jim lived on despite his cancer until 29 November 1989. He was allowed to go to Nancheng and live with his nephew. Then in 1988, when we got the good news that Tommy Yu had been released and was also living in Nancheng, we were overjoyed. Tommy was able to visit Jim and the visits for Tommy must have been invaluable.

The fact that they were able to meet and discuss Church affairs was a beautiful answer to prayer. There they were, two of the players of the 1948 match, together forty years later. And that match was the instrument which, under God, helped to obtain the prayers that brought them together. If you told us in 1948 that such would be the case, we would have laughed heartily, but then our God is a God of pleasant surprises, in my experience.

PRAYER POWER

Regarding the prayer power of our Catholic people, I am reminded of another incident that happened during the persecution. One of our priests was put in jail, and a friend of his at home decided that she would do a holy hour for him each day and would only make one request during the holy hour. The request each day was that the priest concerned would get his night's sleep in the jail in China. Every night for the two years while he was in jail he got a good night's sleep. Not only that, but when he was expelled and living in Hong Kong, his fellow priests could not wake him up. Later, when they took a boat to Europe, they still found it very difficult to arouse him, even aboard ship. The story goes that some of them considered sending a cable to the lady who made the holy hour for him in some words like the following: 'Kindly discontinue holy hour – stop – discontinue – stop'.

Dr Alexis Carrel, MD, and eminent scientist and physician and Nobel prize winner, has written, 'Prayer is a force as real as the gravity of the earth.' That force set in motion by our co-missionaries in different countries kept Jim Yang alive until he got an opportunity of briefing Tommy Yu. That force set in motion by Catholics around the world who heeded and answered Our Lady's appeal at Fatima, brought down the Berlin Wall on 9 November 1989. The prayer power of the devotees of Our Lady of Fatima also brought down the Iron Curtain because she had asked them to pray for the conversion of Russia.

We, who lived under Communism, could scarcely believe that great news on 9 November 1989. In the Communist police state in which we lived, so thoroughly were the people brainwashed, so deeply were they terrorised, that we thought Communism would last for at least a few generations, not only in China but also in Europe and Russia.

What amazed us old China hands was that the Berlin Wall came down more suddenly, unexpectedly and dramatically than the walls of Jericho in Old Testament times. After all, they knew the walls of Jericho were coming down and they were rehearsing for that event. We old China hands knew that Communism carries within itself the seeds of its own destruction. What amazed us was the speed with which it destroyed itself in Russia and in Europe. After 9 November 1989, my hopes for the Church everywhere and for the world are unlimited – although I know many people who do not share them.

Such people are pointing to the fact that the Bamboo Curtain is still intact in China and that there is no freedom there. They are saying the demonstration in Tienanmen Square has not been repeated. Loyal bishops and priests are still suffering in jail. China and North Korea seem to be the last bastions of Communism in Asia. What is needed to put an end to Communism in China and North Korea is prayer power. More frequent and more fervent prayer from each of us.

CHAPTER 15

Our Morale Booster

At this stage of the story, I can well imagine somebody asking, why should we missionaries be totally dependent on foreign prayer power? If, through the power of the Spirit the Church has been set up in Nancheng and the gospel preached there, why should we who are missionaries there have our own native prayer power? Why should we be going round the world with the spiritual begging bowl, as it were, frantically searching for prayers?

That is a very reasonable question to ask and I should answer it like this. In my parish of Kiutu my carrier and gardener, Shong Yung, had an extraordinary gift of prayer. I suppose I am prejudiced, but I think he could outpray anybody I have met in the Western world. He prayed as he walked the ten miles from Kiutu to Nancheng. When he reached Nancheng he went up to the bishop's oratory, and started to pray there with great fervour, and very loudly. On his way back to Kiutu carrying two fairly heavy baskets after his shopping spree in Nancheng, he prayed all the way again. During the day anyhow, like St Patrick, as a man of prayer I would say he was in the marathon class.

Far be it from me to bring a spirit of competitiveness into our prayer lives, but I suppose when we imitate the saints, we in our own little ways try to keep up with them. After my expulsion from my parish on 7 December 1958, Shong Yung's stamina as a man of prayer was brought home to me forcefully. I was interned in the military compound in Nancheng, and it was illegal for him to enter the compound. But each Saturday he ran the gauntlet carrying a little satchel of rice in his hand, visited the church on Saturday evening, went to Mass on Sunday and spent most of the day in the church after Mass. Then he returned to Kiutu.

It was, however, in Nancheng parish that the persecution really hotted up. The Reds made the bishop's parish the target of all their anti-Church, anti-religion activities. In Nancheng they pressurised Catholics into the Patriotic Church. Then using these Patriotic Catholics they started to persecute the cathedral parish, planning to destroy the Church in every other parish in the diocese afterwards. So as far as the persecution was concerned, Shong Yung did not have a big part to play in that city.

But a new man of prayer emerged in Nancheng city, soon after the arrival of the Reds. We who did not know him were not surprised. In the city there were quite a few ex-seminarians, like John McCormack, who had a grounding in theology. One of *them* likely, we thought. It was only when I was summoned by the Commissar to go into Nancheng and answer the charge made against me, namely that I had sabotaged the revolution, that I saw the new man function as a man of prayer.

The bishop had decided to plead my ignorance of the Chinese customs and language as the cause of any mistake that I may have inadvertently made. For that reason he sent his administrator, Barney O'Neill, to the Commissar to answer my charges and to tender an apology. As Barney O'Neill was going down to the Commissar's office, Sr Baptist got a man called Wu Thung Gwa, and sent him to pray before the Blessed Sacrament till Barney O'Neill returned.

Barney did not return for three hours and the atmosphere in the bishop's house was filled with tension as we awaited his return. This was our first encounter with the Communists. Eventually, after three hours, Barney returned and he was ashen pale. But we need not have worried. Thung Gwa's prayers saved me, the bishop had to write a more abject apology, and I was allowed to go back to my parish in three or four days.

The next time I saw Thung Gwa being put on a state of high alert was after Jim Yang had repeated the bishop's sermon of excommunication. In his sermon the bishop had excommunicated the leaders of the Patriotic Church Movement. They had tried to enlist other Catholics into the Movement. To make sure that the bishop or Seamus were not misunderstood, the bishop asked Jim Yang to repeat the excommunication the next Sunday. I was in the back of the church and it was a very moving experience. Jim told them that this sermon that he was now preaching, as he repeated the excommunication, would be his death warrant, and everybody in the church was in tears. Sure enough a day or two later Jim was summoned by the Commissar, and we thought that he would be shot and that we would never see him again. But Thung Gwa, as I said, was on high alert waiting for Jim's call and he again moved into action, praying before Our Lord in the Blessed Sacrament, while Jim was in the Commissar's office. To our great surprise and delight Jim came back in less than an hour.

Of course Thung Gwa was placed in a state of high alert as soon as the Communists started expelling us country priests, and each of us got off lightly, when you consider how priests were punished in other dioceses. We believed that we owed all that to Thung Gwa's prayers. When I think of Thung Gwa's part in the Catholic resistance during the persecution I am reminded of Moses holding up his hands in prayer when his people were at war with the Amelekites, as related in Exodus, Chapter 70. I do not know if Thung Gwa raised his hands while praying before the Blessed Sacrament. I do know that he did raise them when praying in the presence of Our Blessed Lady's statue, and I do know that while he was praying we were saved from the wrath and the fury of the Communists. But who was this Wu Thung Gwa, to whose prayers we owed so much, in those bitter years? I feel the poor man deserves a short biographical sketch here and now.

Biographers are wont to discuss the effect of primary and secondary education on their subjects. We need not delay on such a discussion here, because Thung Gwa never went to school – never mind to the seminary. At the outbreak of the Japanese war he was working in a rice granary near the north gate of Nancheng.

He had been born in a village some distance from the city eighteen years earlier and the name of the village was Mawan. His people were not Christians. When the Japanese dropped a few bombs in that area in July 1942 Thung Gwa was wounded in the leg so that he was unable to walk. He crept on all fours into Nancheng which was a few miles distant, not realising that this was his call to Christianity. At the end of his creep he reached the Catholic hospital, and I know you have already guessed whom he met. Tom Ellis of course.

Tom welcomed him and sent him for treatment to Dr Homberger, who was then the resident doctor, and after a time Thung Gwa recovered. He suffered from elephantiasis, which is a disease that causes the calf of the leg to swell very much. And 'Thung Gwa' means elephantiasis, so he was known as you might say as Elephantiasis Wu. His real second name I have never heard or perhaps I have forgotten it. Soon, however, he became friendly with Tom Ellis and expressed a desire to become a Christian. He was handicapped by the fact that he was a bit deaf and he also suffered from a disease of the scalp. Thung Gwa was a big hulk of a man for a southern Chinese. But he was also so stooped that you did not notice his size except on the rare occasions on which he straightened himself up. He spent some months I presume studying Christian doctrine, and he was baptised as soon as he knew as much about our religion as a man of his mental capacity could hope to grasp. Later Tom Ellis hired him as an understudy for the water carrier in the orphanage and he soon became one of the 'characters' of the compound.

At what stage he came to be regarded by the Catholic community as a man of prayer, in the deepest sense of that word, I do not know. What I do know is that when I was summoned to Nancheng to answer the charge of sabotaging the revolution his reputation was already established. No one except Thung Gwa was considered for the task of interceding for me before the Blessed Sacrament during these tension-filled days.

I cannot remember exactly when I first met Thung Gwa, but what struck me about him on our first meeting was that he had beautiful manners and was the soul of Chinese courtesy.

Whenever he saw a priest approaching he straightened himself up (I think this was about the only time he did straighten himself up), and when the priest got alongside him he would give a fairly solemn bow, smile sweetly and say 'sen fu', (father). I remember one St Patrick's day Peter Campbell, Malachy Toner and I were walking three abreast on our way over to the convent, when we met Thung Gwa. As soon as we approached him, he straightened himself up, stood to attention, and started to bow with vigour, one bow per priest. It seems to me now as if Thung Gwa's head was being bounced off his chest. To get the Thung Gwa 'special' all you had to do was bow to him first, and then he would bow back with everything he had.

Thung Gwa's prayer ministry was not confined to saving us missionaries from being punished for the false charges the Reds had trumped up against us. He was involved in the affairs of the local community at other levels. For instance, in the summer of 1951, there was a drought and the rice crop failed in our locality. Night after night Thung Gwa would get up and pray for a couple of hours before Our Lady's statue in the grotto not far from his room. He would cry to Our Lady and ask her to save the Church, the bishop, the priests, the sisters and the Catholics. His second petition ran something like this: 'Mother of God send us rain and grant that there may be rice to eat.' Joseph Wu, who was then a seminarian and later became a priest and gave magnificent witness during the persecution, informed me during that drought that Thung Gwa continued this night prayer for well over a month.

His prayer was answered and the rain came and fell upon the unjust and the just alike. Joseph Wu, and Tommy Yu, who also later became a priest, told me that when the rain came Thung Gwa kept saying 'Lo yu, lo yu' – 'it is raining, it is raining' to everybody and would point with pride to the rain, as though it belonged to him. Anyhow that is how Joseph Wu and Tommy Yu told me the story, and they laughed heartily as they told it. On the other hand, Thung Gwa had 'prayed his head off' for rain for a month, and who knows to what extent the downpour was not due to his prayers?

Father Faber, a convert of the last century and a popular spiritual director in his day, notes in *Growth in Holiness* that the architectural design of the 'castles we build in the air' can give us a good indication of the state of our spiritual lives. I am not certain that Thung Gwa ever indulged in 'castle building', but if he did I venture to think that the design of the castle was something like this. Thung Gwa on his knees beseeching Our Lady to grant, amongst other things, rain and rice. Our Lady with open hands smiling down at Thung Gwa. In the background torrential rain falling and lush green rice stalks springing up from the brown loamy soil.

The first Sunday morning after my expulsion to Nancheng, I could see that Thung Gwa was also involved in parochial activity. Every Sunday morning he could be seen leaving the bishop's Mass which would be over about 8.30. – he would already have participated in the earlier Masses. Thung Gwa would leave the church in a fairly business-like manner. Some minutes later, he could be seen re-entering the cathedral, a cripple on his back, and the end of a cane in his right hand, and the crook of the cane in the hand of a blind beggar whom Thung Gwa was leading into the church. After depositing the cripple in a seat and leading the blind man to another seat, Thung Gwa would resume his prayers. Before doing so, however, he would look down in my direction with a certain amount of righteousness in his gaze, it seemed to me.

He regarded Tom Ellis as a saint, and when he had first come in contact with the church Thung Gwa would have noticed Tom picking up starving beggars, carrying them on his shoulders into the compound, dressing their wounds and feeding them. Thung Gwa's kindness to the cripple and the blind man each Sunday morning was, I feel sure, due to the influence Tom Ellis had exercised on him. That was the only one of Thung Gwa's parochial activities that I happened to notice, but I fancy that he helped people who needed help at the earlier Masses too, to the best of his ability.

Although some people said that Thung Gwa was not quite the 'full shilling' he had 'big face' amongst the Catholics. My own insight was this, I felt that Thung Gwa was the 'full shilling', especially during inflation, and inflation, like terror and tension, was part of our lifestyle most of the time while we lived under the People's Army of Liberation.

The leaders of the Patriotic Church Movement tried to persuade 'people with big face' like Thung Gwa to join their Movement. The leader accordingly approached Thung Gwa, and threatened him when Thung Gwa refused to join. Thung Gwa worked for the hospital and the leader of the Patriotic Church Movement, the headmaster, assured him that unless he signed up he would lose his job and would have no rice to eat. Although the rice argument appealed very much to Thung Gwa, still he refused to sign the document.

Thereupon the headmaster resorted to a trick. He showed Thung Gwa a list of the names of the hospital staff, and told him he should put his name on that list too. He did not, however, tell Thung Gwa what the list was, and Thung Gwa thought it had something to do with wages, so he made his mark (he could not write his name) on the list. Actually the list on which he made his mark was the list of those who had joined the Patriotic Church Movement, and the headmaster proudly displayed Thung Gwa's mark to one and all. Tommy Yu, the seminarian, told me that the first inkling Thung Gwa had about the headmaster's intentions was when Tommy told him. Thung Gwa got mad when he learned how he had been deceived. He could be seen running round the compound, snorting like an excited buffalo and enquiring diligently about the whereabouts of the headmaster.

That same evening, in January 1952, I was going over to the cathedral to do some work in my capacity as caretaker. When I got halfway, I noticed a crowd had gathered on the verandah in front of the school. Some kind of struggle seemed to be taking place. When I got nearer, it looked as if a rugby football scrum had been formed round one of the pillars of the verandah. The headmaster and some of his henchmen were crouched low and seemed to be pulling someone away from the pillar. Who would it turn out to be do you think, but Thung Gwa? He was grasping the pillar for dear life, and holding his own against three or four who were hanging on to him. For a moment I thought Thung Gwa would pull the verandah, pillars and all, down on himself and the headmaster and other members of the Patriotic Church. Samson, the 'strong boy' of the Old Testament, pulling down the Temple of Dagon on the heads of the Philistines, as narrated in Judges 16:28:30, was the picture that immediately came into my mind.

Still I was rather puzzled at the spectacle. At first I considered it might be some domestic quarrel between Thung Gwa and the headmaster, that had to do with Thung Gwa's duties as water carrier in the hospital. I noticed that 'The Sage', who had tried to take me to the police station a few times since Christmas, and warned me not to interfere in the affairs of the Chinese people, but to keep neutral, was there helping the headmaster. I felt then that neutrality was my best policy, but I also decided that I should be neutral on the side of Thung Gwa, even to the point of sabotage. Deep down I knew that whatever the subject of contention was, Thung Gwa had a hundred to one chance of being on the side of the archangels. I say archangels because I gathered from Tommy Yu that if there was an archangel in the vicinity Thung Gwa would not have much time for a mere angel.

Be that as it may, Thung Gwa was recognised by the Catholic community as our man of prayer and on the many occasions I was called before commissars or party men or chiefs of police, our man of prayer interceded before the Blessed Sacrament on my behalf. On the other hand the Peoples Army of Liberation credited me with being a man of sabotage in the Catholic community. I felt that just as Thung Gwa had used his gifts and expertise to get me out of trouble, so I should use my gifts on his behalf when he was in a spot of bother. So accordingly I cleared my throat, took a deep breath and shouted in a fairly loud voice, 'Thung Gwa, do not heed them, do not take any notice of them.' Apparently I packed quite a few decibels into that shout, judging by its effect.

The effect of my intervention on the headmaster and his assistants was electric – a kind of an electric shock they seemed to get.

Immediately they released their hold on Thung Gwa. Then the headmaster looked around and saw me. He was very embarrassed, I believe, because he had boasted that no force would be used in persuading people to join the Patriotic Church Movement. Now I had caught him red-handed using physical force on poor Thung Gwa for that very purpose. As I have noted Thung Gwa was tricked into putting his mark on the list. Thung Gwa had just erased his mark from the list when the headmaster and his minions came along and man-handled him. But I arrived just in the nick of time, and Thung Gwa did not put on the mark for them a second time. When the headmaster and company released their hold on Thung Gwa they looked rather sheepish, I thought. Thung Gwa shook his head like a swimmer who has just surfaced after a deep dive. Then noticing that it was me, his mate, who had shouted, he gave me a little token bow, not a Thung Gwa special, but with the bow he gave me an archangelic smile.

We have seen how effective Thung Gwa was in his prayer ministry, and how bravely he witnessed to his faith, but his finest hour was still to come. That hour came after the bishop's expulsion. The morale of the whole Catholic community in Nancheng, people and priests, was at its lowest ebb. We were not merely despondent, but also confused. The Communists had given us to understand that Seamus O'Reilly and I would be expelled with the bishop. They changed their minds, however, the day the bishop was departing, although we had said goodbye to all the Christian community. In a prolific rumour producing belt, like Nancheng, it was only natural that the rumour mongers should swing into action. Some of the rumours said that the bishop had been shot in Nanchang, about fifty miles from Nancheng on his way to Hong Kong. Other rumours said that it was farther on in the journey that they killed him. Then the rumours about what would be the likely fate of Seamus and me succeeded the rumours about the bishop, and again the rumours were that we would share the bishop's fate. On the other hand the Patriotic Church Movement, which had trumped up false charges against the bishop and had him expelled, were full of glee. Their morale was at its highest point. They were cock-a-hoop.

But strange to relate, that very evening our morale was considerably boosted and the morale of the Patriotic Church Movement took a nose dive. Here is the story as I dictated it after leaving China. About half past six in the evening of the bishop's expulsion, Seamus O'Reilly and I were washing up after our insipid unsustaining meal of rice. Seamus said to me, 'Did you hear about Thung Gwa?' 'No', said I, 'What about him?' 'Well', said Seamus, 'he is going around repeating, sometimes to himself, sometimes to anyone who will listen to him "shu ssu ken bu ssu", – "the tree is withered but the root is not dead". He has repeated this to the headmaster and his followers and they are hopping mad about it. His words seem to have filled them with remorse; they regard his words as a perfect summing up of the present situation. The bishop of the diocese is expelled, but the Church is far from dead. Probably Thung Gwa has made them feel guilty at having expelled the bishop and having trumped up false charges against him, but that does not stop Thung Gwa from repeating and repeating this proverb.' 'Where did Thung Gwa hear the proverb?' I asked. 'That is what worries them,' said Seamus, 'they suspect someone told him to say it, and told him to taunt them by repeating it. This afternoon they threatened to sack him from his job in the hospital and, when he still continued repeating the proverb, they pulled him out of his room. Then they threw out his 'pee wo' (his blanket) and his belongings and threatened to expel him from the compound. He still insists that nobody told him to say these words.' 'Perhaps he is inspired,' said I half jokingly, but only half. 'It certainly is extraordinary,' said Seamus. 'He sometimes says the wisest things like this proverb, and the seminarians insist that nobody told him or prompted him to do or say anything like that just now. They also say that the loyal Catholics are amused – very amused and delighted at Thung Gwa's intervention, just when it was so badly needed. His intervention came to them as the most pleasant of surprises. They were amazed at the uplifting effect Thung Gwa's words had on them and the demoralising effect they had on the Patriotic Church Movement.'

A diocese suffers a painful bereavement when its bishop is expelled, similar to that suffered in a family when the father dies.

It is a time of mourning in the sense that the flock, the bishop's flock, are in low spirits and downcast. Then Thung Gwa spoke his words of consolation and we all experienced an uplift of heart. 'All boats are lifted by the rising tide.' We had differing opinions about how low Thung Gwa's I.Q. was, but we all agreed that he had 'God's ear' and was very dear to God.

The day after Thung Gwa started repeating the proverb, 'the tree is withered, but the root is not dead', you could see the change in the morale of those of us who were in Nancheng at the time. To a Catholic coming in from the country, the Nancheng Catholics would say, 'Did you hear what Thung Gwa just said?' and repeat the story to them. Reports of Thung Gwa's morale-boosting proverb quickly reached Kiutu, Nanfeng and other parishes in the diocese. Catholics coming in to the hospital from all over the diocese would have known Thung Gwa as a 'character' of the compound and they would bring back the story to their home towns. Everybody seemed to be much more cheerful as a result of hearing the story. With the cheerfulness, one sensed a new surge of hope going through the loyal Catholic community and from Nancheng radiating to the other parishes of the diocese. Thung Gwa, in exercising his ministry of encouragement, had become the diocesan morale booster after the bishop's expulsion.

This was the role for which God chose Thung Gwa at that stage of the persecution. Some would regard Thung Gwa as foolish. Now, forty-one years later looking back at Thung Gwa's contribution, I am reminded of some words of St Paul in his first letter to the Corinthians, Chapter 1 verse 27: 'But God chose what is foolish in the world to shame the wise.' At that point in time I was a fairly young priest and I knew it all and maybe a little more besides. Seamus was equally knowledgeable, if not more so. Paul Yu, a Chinese priest, was brilliant in out-witting the Communists in a typically Chinese fashion. He could be stricken with an instant diplomatic illness, which would wring sympathy from the hearts of the Communists. Yet, there we were, the three of us, feeling empty-handed and uncomfortable, when faced with the problem of boosting the morale of the community after the bishop's expulsion. Of course, Seamus and I did not know from hour to hour what our fate was going to be.

I have dealt with Thung Gwa as a man of prayer, as a witness to the faith and as a morale booster. But what was he like socially, what was it like to know him? When I became a water carrier in the summer of 1951 and shared Thung Gwa's calling, he was anxious to know how I felt about the job and I would share with him any meaningful insights I had acquired. When later I was promoted to the job of part-time pig waiter we would discuss the pitfalls of that profession. Sometimes he would say to me in a rather cautionary tone, 'We must be prepared to die rather than give up our faith.' He was the only man I have seen resisting physically during the persecution, and I have good reason to think that Thung Gwa would resist till death if the need arose.

Every morning after Mass in the convent chapel, he would kneel before Our Lady's statue and pray out loud for some time. Then he would go to the bishop and ask him for his blessing. When he had obtained this he would put his hand on the cape of the bishop's cassock. He would catch hold of the cape of the cassock with his left hand. With his right hand he would point towards the statue of Our Lady looking mildly at the bishop and in a beseeching way say, 'You must ask Our Lady to protect us, to save the Church.' When the bishop had promised him that he would do this, Thung Gwa would release his hold on the bishop's cape. Then he would leave the church and go to his work. Several times the headmaster threatened him that unless he gave up going to morning Mass he would lose his job, but Thung Gwa ignored the threats.

Thung Gwa was about thirty years of age at the time of the bishop's expulsion. He saw the bishop off at the bus when the bishop was leaving Nancheng in December 1952, and I believe he came to the bus with Seamus and me when we were starting our journey to Hong Kong under escort in January 1953. I have never heard anything about him since although I have enquired. Looking back now I am very grateful to God for the contribution Thung Gwa made in the Catholic resistance during the persecution. His words, his inspiring words, revived the drooping spirits of the people. His words were also in a sense prophetic. The root is not dead. In the last forty years it has been fertilised by the blood of Joseph Peng, who died under torture and is regarded by the local community as a martyr. It was also fertilised by the blood shed by John McCormack and Jim Yang when they were savagely beaten and whipped by the Communists. The Church in Nancheng has been renewed and revitalised by the sufferings so many of our people endured during the long and bitter years of persecution.

But the long winter of persecution is now nearly over, and soon the buds will be appearing on the trees. If all this is true and if we did produce men of prayer like the two I have boasted of so shamelessly, another question arises. If we have such prayer power in Nancheng what is the need to go round the globe with the spiritual begging bowl? The answer is this. In the Red persecution, to borrow a phrase from St Paul, our struggle 'was not with flesh and blood, but with principalities and powers, with angels of darkness in high places.' There was a satanic element in Communism. I experienced it. I felt it at least twice. I know it, although I could not prove it for you. To exorcise that satanic element, we needed all the prayers of our co-missionaries round the world. Let us go back ten years before the events described in this chapter to 1942 when Thung Gwa, after having received a wound from a Japanese bomb, crept into the compound in Nancheng. Whose prayers won the grace of the faith for Thung Gwa? I have no doubt it was the prayers of some of our comissionaries out there – God knows where.

PART III

The Legacy of Bishop Cleary

CHAPTER 16

The Drama Producer

The Catholic resistance to the Red persecution so far described took place for the most part within the parameters of Nancheng diocese. In that struggle the Nancheng laity and priests showed a very fine community spirit, and took big risks to support each other. They showed the same do or die *esprit de corp* as their Chinese football team did in the 1948 St Patrick's Day match. In that match Jim Yang, ordained just five years, was the captain, and the leading layman, and man of the match, was John McCormack. Of the seminarians playing that day Joe Peng was ordained to the priesthood in 1952 and other seminarians, Tommy Yu, Joseph Wu and Peter Hsieh, were ordained before Easter 1957.

And now as we look back at their *esprit de corp* during the long bitter years of persecution with heartfelt gratitude, what can we Nancheng Columbans say except 'this has been done by God and is marvellous in our eyes' (Psalm 74). Do they did and die they did, one by one in their struggle for the faith. Eight out of eight of our Nancheng diocesan priests remained loyal to Our Lord, the Pope, the bishop, to the bitter end. Two of them happily are still alive and are functioning as loyal Catholic priests – one of them in Nancheng diocese, Bishop Cleary's diocese.

Their outstanding fortitude during the persecution is a great tribute to their bishop and to the training he gave them. The word *bishop* means *overseer*; the bishop is father of the flock, pastor of the flock, but teaching is his main function. Senator Helena Concannon, in her book *St Patrick: His Life and Mission*, speaks of the paramount importance St Patrick ascribed to the foundation of a native clergy. Patrick Cleary had exactly the same outlook.

THE DRAMA PRODUCER

We have seen the very comprehensive, the very time-consuming training he gave 'our Benignus', Jim Yang. The other seminarians got much the same training. Jim, in his letter to us in 1980, reminds us that even after he had been jailed in 1952 he was allowed out of jail a few times and was allowed to visit the bishop. Each visit seemed to make him more determined to remain loyal to our Holy Father the Pope, till death. He writes of his conviction on this matter as follows: 'This was and ever will be my belief and conviction. To us, everyone of us, the priests of Nancheng diocese, the rebellion against the Holy Father is a deviation from truth – which we will never do, even if we had to lose everything, even our lives. We fought and are still fighting our enemies with the weapon of faith. Even though some died on the farms, or under the hardship of life, the enemies were not able to make us yield to their persecution.' Here Jim is referring to Joseph Peng, who died as a result of torture while he was labouring on a farm. Luke Teng and Paul Yu CM died of starvation while they were working on a farm also. Phil Chou died of starvation in his own house.

Imagine the frustration of the Communists when Jim told them of his convictions about Christianity (just as he has described them in his letter to us). They thought they would be able to brainwash him so that he would join the Patriotic Church. After they had heard him express his convictions, they said he was too badly poisoned by the training and teaching Bishop Cleary had given him on Christianity. The Reds regarded all religion as superstitious and the 'opium of the people'. They would have concluded that Jim was poisoned by that opium. In his letter to us, Jim was speaking for all of our eight diocesan priests in Nancheng diocese. The other seven of our priests would not have been as well educated as Jim because their studies were interrupted by the Red revolution and they had to go to a seminary in south China. Nevertheless Seamus O'Reilly, who has wide experience of giving retreats to priests and seminarians in the United States, said that the education all our Nancheng seminarians got, and their training, compared favourably with the education of seminarians in the Western world.

In the first few sentences of his letter, Jim refers to the debt he owes to Bishop Cleary. He writes 'what a pity that our respected and beloved bishop to whom I owe so much has left us (the bishop died ten years earlier). And how happy he would be to receive this letter from me! Anyhow he is happier still in heaven to see the seeds of his apostolic work are just sprouting well with the help of God's grace.'

It was most unusual for a prisoner to be allowed out of jail to see a friend. I believe it was through the kindness of Mr Sun, chief of police, that this concession was granted to Jim. Mr Sun told me one night during an animated argument that he was brought up a Catholic. I fancy the poor man felt that, by granting this concession, he was helping the Church he had abandoned under presssure. Jim felt that way too. He writes: 'Each time our beloved bishop encouraged me and showed me the brightness of hope in the future. The Church can never be conquered, but in the course of history she always triumphs over her enemies. Christ her divine Spouse conquered once and for all his cruel enemies by his death and resurrection.'

Towards the end of the letter Jim wrote that 'the apostolic work of our most respected and beloved Bishop Cleary has definitely brought forth its fruit.' Our Lord has said by their fruits you shall know them.' I think I know Bishop Cleary better now because of the new light which Jim's letter has shed upon him.

But if Jim Yang's letter gave me a new insight into Bishop Cleary's character, some words of my neighbouring pastor, Luke Teng, were a very unexpected revelation. Luke said to me one day when I was visiting him, 'We Chinese priests of Nancheng Diocese regard Bishop Cleary as the best bishop in China, because he treats us exactly the same as he treats his foreign priests.'

A country with proud cultural traditions and a civilisation reaching back over four thousand years, remembered its defeat by Britain in the opium war 1839 to 1842, when we arrived in China about a hundred years later. So deeply did the educated Chinese feel the 'loss of face' inflicted on them by Europeans that there was a society called 'Know Your Own Humiliation Society' founded by an academic, Kung You Wei, in Peking in 1895. Unfortunately colonialism became associated with religion in the Chinese mind in the nineteenth century, according to Claude Roy in his book, *Into China*. A minister at the court in Peking declared after the opium war, 'China is ready to grant every concession if only the European powers will agree to keep their opium and their Bibles.' Later on the same author writes, 'the English ships from then on disembarked their tons of opium and their Anglican missionaries.'

The Catholic religion also was, in the Chinese mind, associated with French colonialism and the Chinese were quick to tell us that they had been defeated by the French and British between 1856 and 1860 and by the Japanese in 1894. The Communists knew all those facts of history, and indeed accused us of having a share in European colonialism. My little excursion into China's history will help us to understand Fr Luke Teng's mentality.

The Chinese had lost 'face' and had been treated as second class citizens by European colonists. For that reason the priests judged foreign bishops by the way they treated their Chinese priests. On this criterion Patrick Cleary they found perfect. Luke was my neighbouring pastor and he had exactly the same kind of house as I had. He got the same financial help, the same Mass offerings that we got. Whenever he felt the need of a few days' rest he went into the bishop's house where he got a very warm welcome and was made feel at home. Warmth, joy, rest, hope was the atmosphere of that house. Priests from Nancheng parish met priests who were in from the country for a day, or for a few days. It was a Christian community of priests built up by the bishop over the years. In this matter of community building he was a master builder and he was so self-effacing that you failed to notice that it was his work. 'The art of arts is to hide art', said the ancient Latin author. He had that art to a very high degree.

He had another talent which served him well as bishop of Nancheng. When he was rector in the first Columban seminary, he was very interested in drama and often produced the annual play at Easter. He had a sharp eye for the drama in everyday life and could be quite dramatic himself on occasion. I have heard him recite a speech from King Lear with ample gesture and indeed I have heard him recite some of Horace's Odes, some lines from Homer and other classical and modern authors from time to time. All the same, his greatest production was the community spirit amongst the priests in Nancheng diocese, Chinese and foreign – the presbyterate.

He used his gifts as an adequate drama producer to develop that community spirit, but it was generally of the comedy type production – half comedy you could say and half practical joke – that he specialised in. I was at the receiving end of one of these practical jokes and I can assure you it was more than adequate for me. It must have been about March or April of 1949, a month or two before the Communists came, and I was visiting in Nancheng for the day from my parish in Kiutu. There was a good crowd at lunch that day, a number of priests from other parishes were in and at the beginning of the lunch Tom Fisher said, 'There is an air mail letter for you, Luke, from Ireland.' Somebody said that I should open the letter there and then and see if there was any news, and I did this.

To my horror the letter was from the Superior General, Jerry Dennehy and he informed me that he was appointing me as secretary to Monsignor Dooley, who had just gone to Hanoi in Vietnam to be *Chargé d'Affaires*, in the Nunciature in that city. He asked me if I could kindly make arrangements to travel to Hanoi as soon as possible and that he was writing to the bishop about the matter. Well, I was horrified at the appointment, but I knew that the signature definitely was Jerry Dennehy's, and that the letter had an Irish stamp and everything like that. Then the bishop shouted down to me from the top of the table, and said, 'Any news Luke? You look kind of sad I hope it's not bad news.' I told him that it was disastrous news, and all with one voice, looking in my direction, said 'What is it? We hope it is not too bad.' When I said it was a letter from Jerry Dennehy, appointing me secretary to the Nunciature in Hanoi, there was loud laughter and priests, Chinese and foreign, started to congratulate me.

The two Chinese priests, Jim Yang and John Chang, came up to me and said, 'Gungshe Gungshe!' 'Congratulations, congratulations!' Jim joined his two hands together and bowed to me in the Chinese fashion. He bowed his head so low that it was almost a *kowtow* and he moved his hands up and down as he extended his good wishes. John followed suit rather ceremoniously.

When I told them that I would be a disaster in any office into which I might be let loose, someone assured me that there would be plenty of people to do all the office work in a Nunciature. Seamus O'Reilly, though busy with rice bowl and chopsticks, encouraged me by saying that once I got into the diplomatic corps there would be no stopping me. I could only go up. He hoped I would not forget my friends when I came into my kingdom. Then somebody else said that I was probably picked for the job because of my experience in a Communist country and that the Communists were in Vietnam. Another priest remarked, with no great originality I thought, that the appointment just showed you that you cannot keep a good man down.

The bishop, in a serious tone and in his best professorial manner, as he filled his pipe, said how much they would miss me. He explained though that we all get jobs for which we feel we are unsuited and which we think we are incapable of doing well. Actually, he said, that was a much better attitude of mind than the attitude of those who go into jobs with too much confidence. He knew that I would take the job in my stride. Everybody seemed to be laughing and making wisecracks about my new post. When, however, the conversation turned to some other topic, I reflected for a bit. I decided to write to Jerry Dennehy and tell him I was not a 'smooth guy' and, therefore, unsuitable for diplomacy. I would also tell him that I was not cut out to be a secretary to anybody because I was untidy, disorganised and illegible, and then leave it to him.

After the bishop had said grace after meals, I told the company of my decision and then there was a loud peal of laughter. The bishop, laughing helplessly, as he caught hold of my arm, told me that it was a practical joke and that he and Tom Fisher were the perpetrators. After I had given not one, but half a dozen sighs of relief, I joined in the laughter whole-heartedly.

That is one example of the old drama producer at work trying to strengthen the bonds of the community. Tom Fisher was able to forge anybody's signature, and anyone would have thought that it was Jerry Dennehy himself who had signed the letter. Tom Fisher had also got an Irish stamp and put it on the letter and put on that circle that you have round stamps as well. Looking back now, what strikes me most forcibly about that practical joke is that two leading parts were given to the Chinese priests. He had rehearsed with them what they were to do and to say. He wanted to make them feel that they belonged to our community. When we shared our jokes with them we shared everything with them.

Generally I only visited Nancheng for a day, as I did not want to leave the parishioners without Mass the next morning. But even when I was only in for one day, I always left full of Christian hope and encouragement. I was revitalised. In the document on the life of priests, which the second Vatican Council has given us we read: 'All priests who are constituted in priesthood by the Sacrament of Orders are bound together by an intimate sacramental brotherhood. But in a special way they form one priestly body in the diocese to which they are attached, under their own bishop.'

That intimate sacramental brotherhood existed in the bishop's house in Nancheng and the priests visiting brought it with them to the four corners of the diocese, sharing it with their people, who were a 'priestly people'. Baptised Catholics share in the priesthood of the laity. In Article 8 from the same document, we read: 'In this way is shown forth that unity with which Christ willed his own to be perfected in one, that the world might know that the Son had been sent by the Father.'

The local Catholics knew of the unity and brotherhood which existed between the priests. 'Weary Willie', a very gentle courteous Chinese who carried in our rice and vegetables, understood every nuance of every joke, in my opinion, though he did not know any English. He would share his insights with his fellow Catholics. The Chinese were shrewd enough to realise that this symphony of warmth, joy, Christ-centredness, charity, honourable co-responsibility, was subtly orchestrated by the bishop, and that the melody lingered with the visiting priests, like a song in their hearts, when they returned to their parishes.

It was not only the Chinese who felt that there was something special about that community. Peter Fleming, well known author and explorer, mentioned the Columban Mission in Nancheng in his book, *One's Company*. He noted that 'the priests' talk was lit by humour and comprehension, though their lives were in danger from the Reds and their property in danger from the whites, they were daily in contact with misery and suffering of the acutest form, they were worn out by the heat of summer ...' (by the whites, he presumably means the Nationalist soldiers who were fighting the Reds.)

He goes on: 'Yet you would have supposed from their bearing that they were the most fortunate of men, so cheerful were they, so humorously apologetic for the limitations of their hospitality ... theirs were incongruous circumstances in which to find content, yet with them you had the feeling that you were as near to true felicity as you would ever be. I remember them with admiration and occasionally with envy.'

Peter Fleming had travelled widely as an explorer and was not of our faith. He only stayed for one night in Nancheng. For that reason his words about the Christian community, 'yet with them you felt you were as near to true felicity as ever you would be' are all the more remarkable. The year of his visit was 1933 and Patrick Cleary would have only been two years in the country at the time. Also present when Peter Fleming visited were Tom Ellis, Jerry Dennehy, another Columban, and probably a Chinese priest. We who had the privilege of belonging to that community years later would all agree with Peter Fleming, and now in the evening of life we look back with gratitude and nostalgia. The bishop had the rare gift of making all visitors to the Nancheng house, whether laity or visiting priests, feel at home. But a greater gift was that he made his Chinese priests feel that they really belonged to our presbyterate, our community of priests. He trusted them and kept no secrets from them.

One example comes to mind: In the autumn of 1949 Bishop

Galvin, our co-founder and a great missionary, whose diocese of Hanyang was north of the Yangtze river, came to visit us. Bishop Galvin's life, *The Red Lacquered Gate*, by William E. Barrett, has already been written so I will not delay here in telling you about him. What I want to say is that I was in Nancheng from Kiutu just for one night and somebody suggested a game of bridge after supper. Jim Yang was standing in the *chong ha* watching four of us playing bridge when who would come along but Bishop Galvin and Bishop Cleary.

They stood and watched us for a while also. Then they went up to Bishop Cleary's room. Later Bishop Cleary told me that when 'Caw' (Bishop Galvin's Chinese name) saw us playing cards he was not impressed. 'What did he say?' I asked. 'He remarked that Columbans gambling were giving bad example to Chinese like Jim Yang, or words to that effect.' 'What did you say to him?' I asked. 'I just told him that you boys were playing bridge, that it was your recreation and none of my business. Regarding Jim, I said I trusted him, left him to his honour, and that he was a mature priest, though young.' Bishop Galvin disapproved of priests playing cards. (He also disapproved of his priests having radios in his diocese of Hanyang.) He feared that it could give bad example to the Chinese and increase their propensity to gambling.

The question that comes to my mind is how could two bishops, both ordained in Maynooth, have such diametrically opposed views on card playing. The answer as far as I can see is that Father Galvin, when he first came to China, lived and worked with the French Vincentians during his four years of formation in that country. Naturally they would have had an influence on him. Now the French had indulged in a bit of colonialism in China and some of the colonial mentality could have rubbed off on some of the French priests. Their attitude toward the Chinese priests would not have been Bishops Cleary's.

Joe Flynn, who served in Nancheng during the persecution, looked after our affairs in Hong Kong in the eighties. He also helped out as an Advisor in the Diocesan Chancery. He learned that many of the Chinese priests who joined the Patriotic Church were influenced by the colonial mentality of some of their foreign bishops and priests.

The Christian community which he set up amongst the Nancheng priests – the presbyterate – was the rock on which Bishop Cleary tried to build up the Church in his diocese. Our Lord, speaking in St Matthew's gospel, Chapter 7 verse 24, tells us that anyone 'who hears my words and does them will be like a man who builds his house upon a rock.' And Our Lord goes on to tell us that such a house will 'withstand the storms and the floods and the rains which beat upon it'. Our Lord says 'and the rain fell and the floods came and the winds blew and beat upon that house and it fell not, because it was founded on a rock'. In Nancheng diocese the Reds came and they flooded us with their false propaganda and set up a Patriotic Church. They buffeted the Christian Church with the storms of persecution, but the priestly community, which Patrick Cleary had established, stood firm. In fact the bonds of that presbyterate, of that community of priests, seemed to grow stronger as the persecution intensified. To such an extent was this true that Jim Yang, in his letter to us in 1980, says, 'Although we are living in two different worlds, yet our hearts are beating together.' Seamus remarks that this sentence reminds him of the Acts of the Apostles, where we are told the early Christians were one in mind and heart. Neither threats, nor brainwashing, nor whippings, nor torture, nor constant terror over thirty years had weakened the bonds of that community.

Patrick Cleary had listened to Our Lord's voice and followed it when he listened to the voice of his Superior, Dr Michael O'Dwyer, in 1931. The latter was appointing Patrick Cleary to take over in Nancheng district – it was not yet a diocese. Dr O'Dwyer was brief and to the point. 'Pat', he said, 'I am only asking you to do one thing in Nancheng – look after the lads (the priests), because they had it rough under Corney.' Bishop Cleary gave this information to us new arrivals in Nancheng in December 1946. I had forgotten about this incident till Maurice McNiffe reminded me recently.

Patrick Cleary succeeded Cornelius Tierney, who died in the

hands of the Communists while negotiations were taking place for his ransom by Frs Tom Quinlan and Luke Mullany, an Australian Columban. He died on 28 February 1931 and Fr Tom Quinlan later became a bishop in Korea. Corney Tierney was a very prayerful man and full of zeal. He was hard on himself and the priests of the diocese did not find him easy. It is noteworthy that in the short directive Dr O'Dwyer gave Patrick Cleary he did not tell him to try to increase the number of converts or to spend more money on catechists. The priority he was given was to look after the welfare of the priests. Dr O'Dwyer one time said you cannot be a spiritual man unless you are a man first. You have to look after the body in order to be able to pray and to work.

Pat Cleary set about carrying out Dr O'Dwyer's directive of 'looking after the lads' by giving them better food and better houses, insofar as his financial resources would permit. Seven parish houses were built in the years after Pat took over. They were not stately homes. I had no running water, nor electricity, nor telephone, nor gas, nor radio, but I did have a solid stone two-storey house where I could feel at home. At a pinch I could put up three priests, say at the Chinese New Year or at such a time, and entertain them. China is a huge land mass retaining both heat, and surprisingly to us, cold also. The winters were bitterly cold. The stone houses helped to keep out the cold. The charcoal fire I was unable to bear as it got to my throat and nose and so I just wore an extra pair of socks and extra clothes. In summer the stone house was some protection against the deadly tropical heat. Thus the houses that were built made life more tolerable for the missionaries and raised their morale.

Then there was the little matter of food. There was no beef, no mutton, no potatoes available in our part of China, but the bishop worked on what was available. The night we arrived in Nancheng, the eyes popped out of our heads when we saw what was on the menu for supper. Coffee, bacon and eggs and bread. Surely not gourmet fare, you will say! And the popping out of the eyes, was it really necessary? Just listen to Columban Ted MacElroy talking to me about the changes Bishop Cleary had made, since he came to Nancheng fifteen years earlier. We newly arrived missionaries were watching our first meal being brought into the dining room. When I expressed surprise at the lovely meal (I can still sniff the rich aroma of that coffee), Ted began to reminisce. Amongst other things he said, 'I can assure you of one thing. In Corney's time you would not have a meal like that on our table.' But Ted MacElroy never worked under Corney, as he did not come to China until five years after Corney's death. There were, however, seven priests in the diocese who did work under his regime. When they mentioned Corney's name they were very quick on the flaw – all except one of them. Corney is part of our story because I am now dealing with Bishop Cleary and Corney was his predecessor. He is also part of our story because he was captured by the Communists away back in 1930, three years after he arrived in Nancheng. After about four months in captivity he died a very heroic and inspiring Christian death on 28 February 1931. Perhaps this is the place tor me to tell you the story of his captivity and death before I again return to his life in the district of Nancheng.

While Corney was preparing for Mass on 14 November 1930 in the parish of Song Tong Shui, a Catholic came to warn him that the Reds were in town. He rushed out of the church but had only gone a few paces, when two Communists soldiers seized him and pinioned his hands behind his back. Columban, Jim McCaslin, in his book *The Spirituality of the Founders*, tells us what happened next: 'He was brought, pinioned, to the barracks that the local garrison had vacated. He was stripped of his clothes, his hands were bound and he was brutally scourged, the Reds meanwhile mocking him in his sufferings. Afterwards, a soldier placed a red cloak round his shoulders. During all this time he prayed continuously.'

For five days he was kept thus, covered with the red cloak, one hand tied all the time to his body. He looked dazed, according to the local Catholics, and was apparently suffering from an attack of malaria. The local pagans protested against the treatment being given to him. He was a good man they said and was kind to the poor. They shared their rice with him and did their best to make his sufferings tolerable.

On the fifth day he was changed to another place some miles distant, but sprained his ankle on the journey. He was carried on a ladder, but some Catholics procured a chair for him. The Reds handed him over to local bandits and these threatened to kill him in three weeks, if ransom was not paid. He managed to smuggle several letters to his fellow Columbans. His chief request was prayers that he might be able to bear any sufferings that might come to him. He said 'he was quite willing to die for the cause, if God so willed'. He never complained of the very severe Jiangxi winter or the loneliness and sufferings of his captivity in a bandit camp. What he did emphasise was that he was content, thereby showing great patience and great Christian fortitude. Meantime his confrères, Frs Quinlan and Mullany, were making every effort to secure his release by paying ransom. For a time the outlook was favourable. Once, apparently, Corney was freed but after he had journeyed some miles he was captured again. Jim McCaslin writes: 'Hence it was only to be expected that the months of exposure, poor food, of close confinement in some verminous den were bound to weaken him and so, in a way we know not, he died among his captors on the one hundred and eleventh day of his captivity.'

I am indebted to Jim McCaslin for the details of Corney's captivity, and I am also indebted to William E. Barrett for covering the same ground pretty well in *The Red Lacquered Gate*, the life of Bishop Galvin. Before I read those accounts all I knew about Corney was what I heard from the men who worked under him during his three years in Nancheng. They were critical. But they were honest. Now having pondered on his captivity and death the words that come to me regarding Corney are Psalm 116: 'Precious in the eyes of the Lord is the death of his saints.'

Corney had great devotion to the Little Flower and he felt that the Little Flower had shown her special protection for the district of Nancheng. Jim McCaslin writes: 'For the Little Flower was soon to obtain for him a better favour than mere protection, and God's love was to bestow on him a rarer grace than safety. That rarer grace was to enable him to witness to his faith during months of captivity and to state that he was willing to give his life for the cause, if God so willed it.'

All would admit that Corney had reached a high degree of sanctity while he was in Nancheng, though he also had what Cardinal Newman calls some of the 'lingering imperfections of the saints'. I think most of his mistakes and his imperfections were due to the missionary spirituality, which he followed. Corney Tierney inherited this spirituality from Bishop Galvin when he worked in the latter's diocese in Hanyang. Bishop Galvin, in turn, had inherited this spirituality from the French Fathers with whom he worked when he first came to China. It was a French ascetical approach to the apostolate. Corney was 48 when he went to China, and had only one kidney. He worked like 'A Man of Iron'. He was not interested in recreation, rest or vacation. He had been a professor in St Macartan's, Monaghan, and a curate in Ballyshannon prior to that. He was born in Clones Co Monaghan.

In 1931 Corney found himself in charge of the district of Nancheng. That district had one million non-believers within its borders. His duty, as his spirituality led him to see it, was to 'win these souls for Christ.' To achieve this he felt that he and his priests must be perceived by non-believers as men completely detached from moderate creature comforts like moderately good food and moderately comfortable living conditions. He felt, too, that every penny possible must be made available for evangelising, paying catechists, and so forth. The money allocated for priests' maintenance could only buy rather poor food. Now foreign priests, especially young ones – and they were all young – need good food to build themselves up against malaria, typhoid, bubonic plague, dysentery and tropical heat. When moderately good food was not available priests got sick and hospital bills mounted. In one particular year the amount of money budgeted for priests' maintenance in Nancheng was less than one third of the amount spent on hospital bills, according to the priests there.

In 1930 they had up to seventeen priests in Nancheng district. So the French hyper-ascetical spirituality, which Corney inherited from Galvin, did not serve him well in his plan to evangelise the new district. O'Dwyer and Cleary regarded the plan, and the spirituality on which it was based, as too rigorous and impractical. They seemed to belong to a different school of spirituality, if I may so term it. They would be inclined to follow the axiom of St Francis de Sales, 'moderation in all things'. They would recognise that detachment, mortification and asceticism have an important part to play in our lives as Christians. But they would agree with the authors on the spiritual life, who say that mortification must be practised with prudence and discretion. It must never be practised in such a way that it impedes us from carrying out the duties of our state. The French missionary spirituality, which we then inherited, did not meet these requirements.

When I arrived in Shanghai in 1946, I met one of Corney's curates, who sang Corney's praises in high C. He was not from Nancheng. He had been Corney's curate in the diocese of Hanyang, before Corney was appointed Superior of Nancheng district. The priest's name was Bill McGoldrick. He was an Australian and Director of the Region of Asia when I met him. He told me how Corney would make sure that he, Bill, had everything he needed in his room and was comfortable for the night, as he himself would go off to the cold church to adore for an hour before the Blessed Sacrament. It struck me years later that Bill was a kindred spirit of Corney's; he was austere, he did not exude much warmth, he was strict, zealous, prayerful, hard working, thrifty. Some of the priests in Nancheng said that Corney should never have been put in charge of priests and that had he remained in Hanyang, his praises would have been sung in high C by curate after curate. Personally I do not think it would worry Corney very much whether his praises were sung in high C, or whether the priests would be quick on the flaw, when his name was mentioned. In the face of praise or blame, I can see Corney philosophically quoting the Chinese sage: 'If a man speaks of my virtues, he steals from me. If he speaks of my mistakes he is my teacher.' All admitted Corney was a humble man. He had no ambition to be in a position of authority or of honour. I fancy he would have a similar outlook to that of my first pastor in Bristol during World War Two. The latter told me more than once that it was thirty-eight years in purgatory for desiring a bishopric, according to Saint Vincent Ferrer. I forgot to ask the pastor if there would be a remission for good conduct while the culprit was serving his sentence.

Some of the Catholic bystanders in Song Tong Shui said Corney prayed continuously while he was being savagely flogged by the Communists after his capture. When a large scale persecution was unleashed on the district of which he was first superior twenty years later, I am sure he prayed too. He prayed continuously for the priests and the people of Nancheng, who were mercilessly scourged by an ongoing Communist persecution. His powerful intercession, I believe, won for people and priests fortitude and hope, and strengthened their resistance. Like Tom Ellis, he too was 'God's watchman for Nancheng', and his contribution to the spirited resistance of the people, which I have profiled, must be a big one. All our early missionaries made mistakes. They were pioneers, inexperienced, and they were preoccupied with the task of converting China. 'To err is human.' Not only Corney but Bishop Galvin, Dr O'Dwyer, Bishop Cleary, Bill McGoldrick etc also made mistakes. Corney's understandable mistakes helped Bishop Cleary to be a better bishop than he otherwise would have been.

All of us too can learn from Corney. We can learn something about self-sacrifice from that very self-sacrificing man. We can learn something about self-giving because he gave his all. After my China experience, when I was asked what I had learned I came up with the following. Self-sacrifice is of the very core and essence of Christianity. And to the extent that self-sacrifice has a place in our lives, to that extent has Christianity taken root in our souls. But Corney was not the only one of our early members who were ascetical. Bishop Cleary was also ascetical in his own way. For example he stayed twenty years in China without taking home leave. He was very careful to advise his priests to take a rest or to take home leave, but he had that ascetical strain which prevented him from taking a vacation himself. Not only that, but when the 1947 Chapter decided that we Columbans would be entitled to a home vacation every seven years, Bishop Cleary thought that this was a step in the wrong direction and it was a gesture to the prevalent 'cult of softness'. He never drank, even beer on the odd occasions when it was available. We Columbans, who came a generation after the pioneers, made our own mistakes too. However, we have no excuse for repeating their mistakes. George Santayana warns us, 'They who do not remember the past are condemned to repeat it'.

CHAPTER 17

The Teacher

Confucius (551-479BC) was the most famous of all the wise men of ancient China. He profoundly influenced the moral and ethical codes of the Far East. It has been said that the *Sayings of Confucius*, a Chinese classic, has been woven into the fabric of life in Eastern Asian for over two thousand years. However, the followers of Confucius never regarded the Master as a God. He has been revered by his countrymen as the First Teacher, the Sagest of the Sages. Hence it is that the profession of teacher seems to be the most revered of all professions in China. Lin Yutang has this to say in his book, *My Country and My People*: 'China is a land of scholars, where scholars are the ruling class and in times of peace at least, the worship of scholarship has always been sedulously cultivated.' This book was written in the thirties, long before the Communists took over the country. The seminarians and the Catholic community in Nancheng, who had a strong streak of Confucianism in their make-up, esteemed Bishop Cleary a a teacher and a scholar.

He was a very self-effacing man and if you accused him of being a scholar he would deny the charge vehemently in a light-hearted way. Nevertheless when the evidence is procuced I think it would be hard to acquit him of the charge. The evidence, as far as I know it, is as follows. He was versed in all the sacred sciences and had taught most of them. As well as that, he was a classical scholar and very interested in English and Irish literature. But that is not all, he was a man of great intellectual curiosity and tried to keep abreast of what was happening in the world of his day. Apparently he was quite a mathematician too and when the atom was split, he worked out the formula which the scientists used to split the atom.

I was not there at that time, but I do remember one night at the cocoa spree, when we all got together in the dining room to imbibe some cocoa at 9.00p.m. at night. It must have been fairly potent cocoa, when one remembers the animated discussions that took place during that hour, and the discussions seemed to get more animated after the second cup of cocoa. The night I have in mind must have been some time in 1950 because a new book by Professor Albert Einstein, the great scientist, was published that year.

That evening somebody raised the question of Relativity which was discovered by Einstein earlier. The bishop, in his capacity as amateur physicist, explained Relativity to us. I can see him now as he sat at the head of the table, stand up and take a tangerine or something like that in his right hand, swing his right arm backwards and then forwards, as if he was throwing something into space. This gesture had to do with Relativity. It is not true to say that all I know about Relativity could be written on the back of a stamp. But that night all I was able to contribute to the discussion was a relevant Limerick which I had heard in Bristol City during World War Two. It goes like this:

> There was a young lady called Bright
> Who travelled much faster than light.
> She set out one day
> In a Relative way
> And returned on the previous night.

He believed that his priests should be educated men, and there he was giving us ongoing education in an informal way, while we were under the influence of cocoa. Another night he mentioned a recent encyclical about the Church by Pius XII. I believe it was called the 'Mystical Body of Christ'. I grasped at his words on the encyclical as a drowning man grasps at the proverbial straw. The reason I did this was that I was in the seminary that year and teaching a boy, the senior boy in the seminary, about the church. The bishop encouraged everybody to join in the discussions and everybody found them very enjoyable.

But the main task he set himself, 'after he had looked after the lads', was to teach and train and ordain more Chinese priests. 'The aim of the church in the missions can be expressed in a single idea – the raising up of a native clergy', wrote Bishop Frank Ford, a Maryknoll missionary whose diocese was south of us, and just north of Hong Kong. Our neighbouring Vincentian American bishop agreed with Bishop Ford and Bishop Cleary on this matter.

Some of the French bishops were slow to ordain a convert. Some of them felt that Chinese priests should come from families who were true to the faith for a few generations – had proved themselves, so to speak. Bishop Galvin, who had been with the French Vincentians for four years, did not make the establishment of a native clergy his first priority. Bishop Galvin's priority seemed to be to baptise in as large numbers as possible, and of course there was a school of thought behind this attitude. I remember Bishop Cleary had an equation which went something like this. From the point of view of preaching the gospel to the Chinese, one good Chinese priest is more valuable than a thousand converts. In my opinion, Bishop Ford was the bishop Patrick Cleary admired most in China. Ford also wrote 'preaching the gospel is the first duty of the apostolate; but it is merely in time, not in importance. The most important duty is to lay the foundation for a permment indigenous church. We are in mission countries, not to settle down indefinitely as indispensible for the expansion of Christianity, but to build a nest for the fledgling native clergy, who will one day replace us.' Ford goes on to say that recent Popes had again and again reminded missionaries of their ultimate goal.

Bishop Cleary did not need to be reminded of what that ultimate goal was, and nobody was more anxious than he was to build a nest 'for the fledgling native clergy, who would one day replace him.' But in spite of his enthusiasm, he was five years in China before he could build the nest. He tells us in a synopsis of events in Nancheng during his time, that it was not until 1936 that the training of seminarians could be seriously undertaken. It was only by that time that the primary schools were beginning to bear fruit. He had built seven Catholic primary schools which would be nurseries for the seminary, in the five years since his arrival, thus laying the basis of a Catholic school system. Again in this matter of Chinese primary schools, there were other bishops in the country, including Bishop Galvin, who did not agree with him. I understand, however, Bishop Galvin changed his mind in later years.

Bishop Cleary wanted an educated laity. As well as being a nursery for the seminary, the Catholic schools would send some boys and girls to middle school and these later became teachers, nurses or whatever. In the parish of Kiutu, where I was pastor, all the teachers had got their primary education in one of the schools Bishop Cleary had built. His plan was to have an educated Catholic laity in his diocese, who would bring Christian values into the professions, into the business world and into local government. This was his aim. He wanted responsible, trustworthy Chinese citizens to come from his Catholic schools.

News that the bishop's aims in Catholic education and his views on the subject had been achieved and justified, reached us long after the bishop's death. It happened like this. Fr Peter Hsiu (who scored the winning goal for the Chinese on St Patrick's Day 1948) visited China about 1980 from Fiji, where he had helped the Columbans in that country as a missionary. During his visit to China he was told that the Catholics had a great reputation in the jails, labour camps and communes for trustworthiness, honesty, reliability, wherever they worked. Indirectly the bishop's policy and the policy of our neighouring American Vincentians, Bishops Quinn and O'Shea, on education were bearing fruit and a very favourable image of the Church was being projected in the province of Jiangxi.

Before I return to the Nancheng seminary, which started in 1936, let me put on record here, that the arrival of the Columban Sisters, on St Patrick's Day 1935, must have been an inestimable blessing to the bishop and to the diocese. It must have encouraged him to go full speed ahead with setting up Nancheng seminary. The arrival of the sisters must have given an enormous boost to the morale of the diocese, because they helped in the hospital, in training cooks for the priests in the country, and also in working as catechists. When you consider that the seminary was only started in 1936 and had to close down in 1948, you will get a pleasant surprise to hear that there were ten priests ordained for the diocese of Nancheng who started in Bishop Cleary's seminary. They did not all finish there, because the Communists interrupted their studies. According to Harold Watters, a Columban who worked in Hanyang, Bishop Galvin had three priests ordained in his seminary. Actually, the junior seminary was in Hanyang, and Bishop Galvin had some Chinese priests who worked in the Hanyang district before his arrival. He also had a few priests who were ordained in Rome, in the Propaganda College. I am unable to get the exact figures, but it does seem that although Hanyang had six times as many Catholics as Nancheng, Nancheng had more native priests ordained.

But what was the atmosphere of the Nancheng seminary like? I was there for the last year, 1947 to 1948, and my testimony is that the atmosphere there was very like the atmosphere of the Columban seminary where I was trained in Dalgan Park, Galway. Patrick Cleary was the first Rector of that seminary. As a teacher, professor, he had unrivalled experience. As a young priest he taught seminarians in Maynooth for Ireland and indeed for the English-speaking world. In Dalgan he taught Irish, American, Australian, New Zealand, English, and Scottish seminarians, who were destined to become missionaries in China. In his late fifties he faced his most daunting challenge, namely the teaching and training of Chinese seminarians to become secular priests for the diocese of Nancheng. But he loved challenges. As a teacher he learned from each challenge and his experience in Dalgan helped him immensely in the seminary in Nancheng. What he aimed to do was to transplant that seminary into Chinese soil with its spirit, charism, formation, warmth, joy, honour system, the lot. I have described the type of formation Tom Ellis got in the chapter 'Columban Missionary'.

From my observation during the year in which I was attached to the seminary in Nancheng, I would say that the seminarians got exactly the same formation as Tom Ellis got when Bishop Cleary was his Rector and his professor. There was a slight difference, and it was this. Bishop Cleary made no attempt to make the

Chinese seminarians Columbans, he just wanted to make them high quality diocesan Chinese priests for the diocese of Nancheng. The fact that he and all of us Columbans are secular priests may have helped him to achieve his aims. He respected their Chinese culture.

Pat Gately, an American Columban, was Rector of the seminary when I was there, but in fact Bishop Cleary was the overseer of the seminary, as he was of the diocese. You could say he ran both. Training young seminarians kept him boyish even in his sixties. In every aspect of the seminary he was interested and involved. In my memory I can see him on a morning in spring, standing in front of five or six of the junior seminarians. If you do not mind, he was teaching them P.T., physical exercise! He had Indian clubs in his hands, swinging them back and forth and teaching the young boys to do the same. The physical exercise class took place on the verandah outside the bishop's room.

The nickname Mike Halford had for the bishop, when he was talking to me, was 'the Old Eagle'. Now I see there was something in that nickname when I consider how he watched over the 'nests he had built for his fledgling native clergy'. Verses from the canticle of Deuteronomy come to mind:

> Like an eagle that watches its nest
> that hovers over its young
> so he spread his wings.

The eagle is, I suppose, the overseer *par excellence*.

Bishop Cleary had an easy relationship with even the youngest of the seminarians. He could identify with them, and this was another of his gifts. They spoke to him in English, because they wanted to become proficient at that language, and they would confide in him their problems and difficulties. When I think of the pleasant place Nancheng seminary was, I am reminded of something written by Pádraig Pearse, the educationalist: 'The bringing together of pupils in some pleasant place under the fosterage of some man, famous among his people for his greatness of heart, for his wisdom, for his skill in some gracious craft – here we get the two things on which I lay the most stress in education: the environment and the stimulus of a personality which can address itself to the child's, to the pupil's worthiest self.' In Nancheng seminary we had the pleasant place. It was under the fosterage of a very educated man, and the stimulus of his personality addressed itself to each seminarian's worthiest self. Pearse founded a school, St Enda's, in which he put into practice all that he has written about education. The school ran on the honour system just as Dalgan did. Bishop Cleary, writing in *The Far East* magazine, says that when Fr Blowick was travelling through Ireland by train, trying to get the Society off the ground, he carried with him, as his *vade-mecum*, *The Story of A Success* by Desmond Ryan. The success in question was the success of St Enda's school from which John Blowick borrowed when he was setting up the first Columban seminary.

I often heard Bishop Cleary say John Blowick was the man with the vision. John Blowick was the man who saw that it would help him in training priests for China to bring some of the spirit of St Enda's, like the honour system and so forth, into the seminary he hoped to acquire in the near future. But Bishop Cleary, the first Rector, was the man who implemented that system, as I have said, in Dalgan and also in Nancheng.

I have already dealt with the quality of Chinese diocesan priests Bishop Cleary's seminary system produced in China. There were, however, four other priests who started in Nancheng seminary, but had to leave the country when the Communists came, and they were ordained in Genoa. They too were high quality priests.

Two of them, seeing that they could not return to their own country, helped the Columbans as missionaries in Fiji Islands, Peter Hsiu and Joseph Weng. One of them died very young, Peter Chow, and the other, Peter Yü, has been in Taiwan all his life. By the way Joseph Weng joined him in Taiwan, after a short period in Fiji.

The surprise is that 'the Old Eagle' was able to run the diocese as well as run the seminary. He was not able to rush about from parish to parish and to visit every out-mission like Bishop Galvin did. He went to the parishes for Confirmations and knew everything that was happening in each parish. He had all the time in the world for each pastor who visited Nancheng, and enquired about everything. He said he trusted his priests and he also encouraged and affirmed them each time they visited him.

I fancy, too, that Bishop Cleary felt that priests liked their bishops better when they were a safe distance from them. He would have heard the story which Australian, Gerry O'Collins, told us as seminarians, a story which applied to a number of dioceses in China apparently. Gerry was a priest of Hanyang diocese. He told us that the highest happiness to which a priest could aspire, after he had his day's work done, was a good lamp, a good book, and a good distance from the bishop.

On the other hand, Bishop Cleary was criticised by his own priests, not only for giving too much time to Jim Yang, but also for giving too much time to the other seminarians. All his life, you could say, was spent training boys for the priesthood. It was the job he liked best and did best. Though passing the torch to the seminarians was his *forte*, he did not neglect his other episcopal duties.

One of his contemporaries told me that Bishop Cleary had the reputation of taking an unorthodox approach to problems, but that somehow or other his approach worked well in the end. In retrospect now it is hard to see how he could have prepared his diocese more effectively for persecution, than by training the excellent priests whose witness I have described.

But as well as the priests, there were also quite a few catechists around the diocese, like John McCormack, who had spent some time in the seminary, and who were a great bulwark against Communism and against the Patriotic Church when the persecution came to their parishes. I think I know why Bishop Cleary's unorthodox approach to many problems seemed to work out well in the end so often. Ted McManus, who was bursar when we arrived in Nancheng, gave me that answer. He told me that each day Bishop Cleary offered his Mass for the spiritual welfare of his diocese. He offered it, through the hands of Our Lady of The Rosary, who was patroness of Nancheng Cathedral and of

Nancheng diocese. Seeing that this story is about Catholics in Nancheng diocese who found themselves involved in the Catholic resistance during persecution, I should ask what was Bishop Cleary's contribution? It was incalculable. In one way or another he touched the lives of most of the people involved in the resistance in Nancheng diocese with whom I have dealt up to now.

And, when I speak about his contribution, I am thinking only of his contribution as a teacher, which was mainly made through the seminary. But when the persecution did come how did he handle the situation as a bishop? I must confess that I often criticised his handling of particular instances, after the Reds came. I felt sometimes that he had been too accomodating with the Communists. Looking back now, however, with the gift of hindsight, I see that he was not easy on the Reds, but he was flexible when principle was not at stake. When principle was at stake he was unyielding.

We knew what he expected of us at each stage of the Communist take-over and the persecution that followed it. He had a plan for us. The plan was that each of us was to stay at his post, and if he had to go on the run, to run inside the parish. He sent each of us a brilliant paper on the history and the aims and the philosophy of Communism. We knew what we were up against.

When we country priests got permission to visit the bishop in Nancheng occasionally, he always encouraged us and discussed our difficulties with us. My big difficulty was that I seemed to be the first to get into trouble with the Communists, and that they had charged me with sabotaging the revolution and with other forms of sabotage, while other priests in the diocese did not have any such problem. I had guilt feelings that I was bringing trouble on the diocese, because each time that they charged me they referred the matter to the bishop. When I asked him for advice on this difficulty which I had, his advice was something like this. You are the man on the spot. As each crisis comes up, you make your own decision, following the best information available. If subsequently it turns out that you did not make the best possible decision, do not worry, I will back you to the hilt. Such advice was very helpful, gave one confidence and helped one to realise that co-responsiblity about which we were taught in the seminary was something that the bishop practised in his diocese.

Of course, when we visited him after the Reds came, we also had the cocoa sessions at nine o'clock. However on such occasions the sessions were mostly about the problems that the different priests had, and what the Reds might do next in a particular parish or in a particular diocese. They were enjoyable, these cocoa sessions, and after the second cup of cocoa we forgot about our problems and there was a lot of mirth and laughter. There was also a little subtle ongoing education for us each time that we visited him. His views on so many things were original.

As I have admitted, I criticised him on various counts during the Red occupation and the persecution afterwards. Looking back now from this distance of time I believe I was mistaken, and feel that he handled the many crises which were part and parcel of day to day living during our years under the Communists with intelligence and skill. He looked forward to the coming of the Communists with dread. He told Maurice McNiffe that he had a rough time under the Japanese, that he had no holiday for about twenty years, and that he did not feel up to the strain which Communism would bring. Still he never panicked during the ongoing ordeals which the People's Army of Liberation brought with them. He retained an inner peace and an outward calmness and quiet trust, which was an example for all of us.

To my mind the man who profited most from the bishop's informal ongoing education scheme was Tom Ellis. The bishop never claimed this, nor did he ever hint at it, but as I have said he was a very self-effacing man. I believe he helped Tom very effectively on the road to holiness by giving him a deeper understanding of the breviary and of the psalms in particular. Let me quote from Bishop Cleary's letter to Dr O'Dwyer in which he told the latter that they all believed in Nancheng that Tom was a saint. He writes 'What?, the Tom Ellis whom we used to know?' 'Yes; the very same – the very ordinary, perhaps in most ways under average, Tom Ellis whom you and I knew as a Dalgan student and a young Columban priest; the very same grown up, matured, mellowed, mortified, exhausted, dead on the field of honour!' The bishop continues: 'What happened? Simply this: there was always a fundamental greatness, had we known it. God did the rest.' It always amuses me when I read that paragraph. I have described the gifts of Tom Ellis, the gifts of hands and head and heart which God had given him. Then if Tom was under average, the big mistake the Columbans have made is that they did not look for more under average men like Tom Ellis.

However, we must not forget that that letter was written from one academic to another, one professor to another. I think Dr O'Dwyer had taught Tom philosophy. I imagine too that Tom might not be able to give a bright answer to some of the more profound questions of philosophy, as we were taught it. I agree with Bishop Cleary when he says that God did the rest, but I would like to add that God was helped by Patrick Cleary.

Even if Tom were a well above average missionary it would be very hard to imagine him out there in China, studying Hebrew in order to get a deeper understanding of the psalms, unless he had been encouraged and helped to do this. I think it was Cleary's example, above all, that encouraged Tom to acquire a fine knowledge of the Old Testament, and to attempt to recover his Greek from the New Testament.

The bishop assured us in his letter that Tom did attempt these difficult studies in spite of his other heavy commitments in Nancheng. The bishop goes on to say: 'He might at any moment appear with a volume of Augustine, or Aquinas or Bossuet, and a request to 'listen to this'. He might spend an hour studying his Office before he read it. Even the brighter than ordinary missionary does not undertake such tasks unless he has a lot of encouragement and the stimulus of a personality behind him and also the example. I feel Bishop Cleary provided not only the stimulus and encouragement but also the example.

Let me tell how I discovered the diligence and devotion Bishop Cleary put into praying the Divine Office fervently. He was always quoting from the psalms or indeed from other parts of the Bible at the cocoa sessions, when the quotation would be relevant. I opened his breviary a number of times in his oratory in Nancheng, and discovered that he had written in pencil, at the beginning of each psalm, something that might help him to recite the psalm more prayerfully. The words might be about the origin of the psalm or about the author (if the author were known) or about what sentiment the psalm evoked in him.

It should be noted that in those days we prayed the breviary in Latin. His devotion to the Office was contagious, and even I caught a very mild form of that contagion, so that I began to write words at the beginnings of the psalms in my breviary. And I believe that Tom Ellis caught a lot of it. I believe Tom belonged to the same school of spirituality as the bishop. He was not only his disciple but they both shared a nobility of character, a certain gallantry and compassion. As well as that, although Patrick Cleary had studied scripture for so long, he was always trying to improve his knowledge of the psalms. He felt that the psalms and the other readings in the Divine Office provided the missionary with everything he needed for his personal prayer, meditation, preparation for Mass, spiritual reading, etc. The bishop writes: 'I think his formal prayer to the end was simply a devotional consideration of the Divine Office, and the only 'lights' he got were such as were derived from a more thorough assimilation of the wisdom contained in its psalms and lessons.'

But even from his early years as a priest, Tom seemed to get remarkable spiritual assistance from praying the Office. The ordinary young priest found saying the Office in Latin a bit of a burden. Tom, on the other hand, writing in his spiritual notes of November 1939, had this to say: 'On occasions like this, when I intend to turn over a new leaf, it usually happens while I am saying the Office.'

From my little experience, it is easy for me to understand how Tom Ellis began to imitate Bishop Cleary's example in trying to understand and love the Office better and to recite it more fervently. In so far as the Office helped him to become holy, then I charge Bishop Cleary with being an accomplice, being Tom's accomplice in this matter of attaining sanctity, and they all claimed that Tom had attained to quite a degree of sanctity.

In his letter to Dr O'Dwyer, Bishop Cleary says not a word, gives not a hint, that he helped Tom to reach the 'heights', but then that is the kind of self-effacing man he was as I have mentioned more than once in this story. If he heard a priest were writing an article for the *Far East* magazine, he would express an interest and would help the priest to improve it, but would not mention the matter to anybody else. The bishop was an accomplice first of all by example, and then by word. Tom was with the bishop for the last seven years of his life, from 1938-1945, and so he had a long time to be enriched by the bishop's ongoing education. Especially with regard to the breviary.

But I have another reason for making this charge against the bishop. When he asked me to join the Seminary staff in 1947, I just laughed and said that I was a tyro at the Sacred Sciences, and when he only laughed at that I thought I would play my strongest card. I said I had missed a year in the seminary, had only done three years' theology on account of a burst appendix. I added that I had tried to make up the missed year during my last year, but that I really never got a chance to do the psalms, as the year I missed was the year that the Professor was doing the psalms. He only laughed some more and we left it at that. However he did not forget it.

Four years later, I was sitting in my room on a morning in January 1951, waiting in great suspense to be summoned for my trial. Mick Moran and I were waiting day after weary day. The bishop, when he came into my room had a book. The book, newly arrived from the States obviously, was called *The Psalms: A Prayer Book*. On the left side of each page was a new Latin version of the psalms, translated from the Hebrew by the professors of the Biblical Institute. On the right of the page was an English translation. The book was approved by Pope Pius XII. Before each psalm, there were a few words about the theme of the psalm and its authorship, much the same thing as the 'old producer' had been doing in his own breviary but more elaborately. As well as that there was a prayerful reflection at the end of each psalm and a few sentences of commentary. He laughed as he left the book on the table of my room, and assured me there was no need for me to be a tyro any longer as far as the psalms were concerned.

I studied the psalms in the book he gave me, a few hours each day, and my studies were a voyage of discovery. Persecution is a great teacher. Persecution seemed to make the psalms so relevant; we were being pursued, falsely charged, plotted against. But the psalms taught me that our God was our rock, our refuge, our shield against the enemy, our shepherd who looked after us even as we walked 'through the valley of darkness'. Bishop Cleary would come in sometimes, and we would talk about some difficulties I had with a particular psalm and he was most helpful. In his letter to Dr O'Dwyer, Bishop Cleary had mentioned that any 'lights' that were given to Tom came to him through a prayerful recitation of the breviary. The psalms as I studied them shed new light on our situation. For me they shed new light on God's goodness and his love for me, and his desire for my love in return, and the place of persecution in his plan, and the part he expected me to play during the persecution. Some of the psalm verses gave me light to see 'God's plan, reaching from end to end, mightily ordering all things sweetly.'

Scott Fitzgerald, my favourite American author, has put into words the way I felt, when a psalm verse would throw a new light on God or on some of his attributes. Here are the words: 'One of those immortal moments which come to us so radiantly that their remembered light is enough for us to see by for years.' Such moments came to me from time to time as I studied the psalms, pending my trial as a criminal. Has not the psalmist, himself written:

> Thy word is a lamp to my feet,
> A light to my path.

The gifted novelist (and the words are taken from his novel *The Beautiful and the Damned*) is able to put into words what we deeply feel but are unable to describe. But the lights given to us by some psalm verses is sufficient for us to see by, not merely for years, but for life. And I personally feel when my eyes are no longer able to read the breviary and when my hands are no longer able to lift it, some of those friends amongst the psalm verses will stay with me to sustain me, to bring me light, happiness and peace. I think, therefore, I have proved my point that the bishop was an accomplice to making a saint of Tom Ellis, because Tom was seven years with the bishop.

In charging the bishop, 'The Teacher', with being a scholar, I omitted one important piece of evidence. As well as his erudition, which I have already mentioned, the bishop was also a competent writer. He never spoke about the craft of writing, a craft which he had mastered, except once in my recollection. He said to me one day, 'Wattie McDonald gave me a start in life.' He was referring to Dr Walter McDonald, who was a professor of theology in Maynooth and had taught Bishop Cleary as a student. Bishop Cleary went on: 'Wattie taught me to say whatever I had to say with clarity and simplicity.' It is noteworthy that at the Blowick Centenary in 1988 Monsignor Micheál Ledwith, the then President of Maynooth, quoted Wattie McDonald as saying something like this: 'I thought there was no life left in Maynooth until I saw Maynooth men start the Maynooth Mission to China.'

Bishop Cleary was capable of doing some beautiful descriptive writing, and here is an example of it. I quote from *The Far East* of August 1938 where the bishop is describing the province of Kiangsi: 'Kiangsi is beautiful. Take a dozen Connemaras or Killarneys, or a few slices of the Rockies, juggle them about in a sweepstake drum, and pitch them forth in hills and mountains, now by the dozen, now by the thousands, anywhere, everywhere, shouldering one another, calling to one another, on top of one another, and then you will have something of the ground plan and specifications of Kiangsi.' (In Bishop Cleary's time it was spelt 'Kiangsi.' The Communists have changed the spelling to 'Jiangxi'.) 'Next procure all the water of the Amazon and send it laughing, splashing, dashing, flashing down your mountain valleys, even as the waters come down in Lodore, catch as much as you can of it once more and turn it into a thousand rice fields a mile up in the air – fields as flat and as small as a tennis court – send it along, terrace after terrace to join the brooks below; seek out and plant all the semitropical vegetation you can find; borrow some millions of azaleas and sow them broadcast across the hills, making them peep out at you from every hillock; and then like the Lord look upon your work and you will see that it is good.'

THE TEACHER

There you have it, a highly imaginative piece of descriptive writing, a kind of a prose poem. I find in it echoes of two poems, Southy's 'The Cataracts of Ladore' and Belloc's 'Tarentella'. I would not be able to write like that in a thousand years, but I am afraid I have to confess that I never thought our local Jiangxi scenery was so beautiful. I have always been more interested in people than in places, and the bishop told us to watch out in our early years for customs and traditions that we, as foreigners, thought strange and bizarre, to watch out for them amongst the people. By the time I had finished that, the Reds had come and again under the People's Army of Liberation, I am afraid I was more interested in survival than in scenery. Presumably the bishop wrote this piece shortly after he arrived in China, while he still would notice things with the eyes of a newcomer. He liked his articles to be published as he wrote them and he was not pleased when editors tampered with them.

A booklet into which he put much labour was what he called his 'transcommentation' of the gospels. He translated the gospels from the Latin into English and in the translation he added little bits of commentary here and there. His object was to make the gospels as intelligible as possible for the seminarians, without burdening them with too much detailed commentary. In this he succeeded; the seminarians were very well grounded in the scriptures and this must have been a great help to them during the persecution. As I have noted earlier, the bishop felt strongly that St Paul had written three letters to the Corinthians and that the last letter could be reconstructed from passages that were out of place in the two letters we possess. He set out to reconstruct the third letter and often asked me to have a look at his job of reconstruction. 'I have the crossword puzzle type of mind', he used to say to me with a laugh, and this was the only recreation he took as far as we could see. This job of reconstruction? He sent the finished work to the late Monsignor Kissane, a scripture scholar in Maynooth, and the latter sent it to the Biblical Commission. They published it in a specialist scriptural magazine, but they said that his reconstruction was too subjective.

After he came back from China, I suggested to him more than once that he should write his autobiography as his life covered a very interesting period of history, not only in China but also at home. However, he elected to take some classes and teach the seminarians instead. In his young days he had written a pamphlet called *The Maynooth Mission to China*, about the beginnings of our Missionary Society. For his Doctorate of Divinity, the thesis he chose was 'Usury'. Believe it or not, I saw a priest reading it in 1993, but I must confess that I have never read it myself.

His work amongst the people and priests of Nancheng diocese in peace, no less than in persecution, is his biography from 1931-1952. I think that, like his beloved St Paul, he would have shirked from writing an autobiography lest he might appear to be commending himself. St Paul, in his second letter to the Corinthians, writes: 'Are we beginning to commend ourselves again? You yourselves are our letter of recommendation, written on your hearts to be known and read by all men, and you show that you are a letter from Christ delivered by us, written not with ink but with the Spirit of the living God, not on tablets of stone but on tablets of human hearts.'

CHAPTER 18

Back to our Roots

Although Bishop Cleary did not give us the story of his life as a missionary, he has given us a fascinating glimpse into the beginnings of that story. The article entitled 'Beginnings Remembered' was written in the October issue of the 1966 *Far East*. Bishop Cleary was eighty years of age when he wrote it. He not only recalls the circumstances which led to his joining the Maynooth Mission to China, as the Columbans were then known, he also recalls the beginnings of that society, which he joined while he was a professor of theology in Maynooth. Looking back now it seems strange to me that an idealist like Pat Cleary did not join until April 1918, two years after the society started. When it did start, in 1916, idealism, as I have noted, was running at high tide all over the land. In the article, Patrick Cleary confessed that he felt excited, full of wonder, and a little vulnerable and uneasy, when the news first broke. John Blowick, his fellow professor in Maynooth, told him he was resigning his Chair of Theology and joining with a priest called Edward Galvin, who had spent four years in China, in an effort to launch a missionary movement for the conversion of China. My own recollection is that John Blowick, when giving us talks in the seminary, told us he wrote to Patrick Cleary asking him to join the little missionary movement in Dalgan Park, because he needed him to be Rector of the new seminary. However there is no mention of this in 'Beginnings Remembered'. What is highlighted is the long session he had with John Blowick on the eve of ordination day in Maynooth in April 1918. John Blowick brought his five senior students to have them ordained in Maynooth in April 1918, because there was a scare that Lloyd George, the British Prime Minister, would bring in a conscription act whereby only ordained priests would be exempt.

Patrick Cleary writes: 'The ordination day marked a turning point in my life. Father Blowick drew a very pathetic picture of the shortage of priests in Dalgan Park with special emphasis on his inability to replace Father Ned McCarthy, who was being sent to the States to start the society there. He made, as far as I remember, no suggestion that I should resign my chair and join him, but Padraig Connolly, a rabid Gaelic Leaguer and a fervid idealist, who recently had been appointed assistant bursar in Maynooth, pounced upon me (they were classmates) with an eloquent and insistent demand that I go at once as it was my duty to do so. Wearily I agreed to think it over during the night and promised that they would see me in the organ loft of the chapel during the ordination ceremony, if I agreed to go.'

Notice Patrick Cleary did not say that he would give them a yes or no answer in the morning. Why? Because as I have told you, in the chapter 'A Picture To Remember', he was a man of signs and symbols. I suppose he became this type of man from his intensive reading of the Old Testament. You remember the Irish blackthorn he gave to Jim Yang twenty five years later. It was a sign of the authority he was vesting in Jim and a symbol of the *Bacall Íosa*, (crozier of Jesus), which St Patrick gave to Benignus.

Anyhow the bishop continues in his article: 'Was it folly or grace, or was it *esprit de corps* that drove me to the organ loft that morning?' Personally I would say there was the grace of God and there was *esprit de corps* in helping him to arrive at his decision, but as an old China hand I detect another factor. He speaks of Padraig Connolly, who afterwards joined our missionary society, as 'pouncing on him, battering down his defences'. As I now picture Patrick Cleary on that April morning, the flaming torch in his hand in the organ loft, I ask myself if he were not gently and subtly shanghaied into becoming a China hand. Or was he hijacked? But the decisive factor I believe was the admiration he had for John Blowick and their friendship. I have heard Patrick Cleary say more than once that in matters pertaining to our missionary society J. B., as we called him, our co-founder, got 'special lights' from God. He also regarded J. B. as a man of vision. J. B. certainly had the vision to see that Pat Cleary was the ideal man for Rector in Dalgan Park. He had the ideal temperament for training seminarians for missionary work in China. He had the gentlemanliness, the ongoing boyishness, the ability to relate on equal terms with his seminarians which won their confidence. But, man of vision though J. B. was, I doubt if he could have foreseen that April morning in 1918, that thirty-two years later Patrick Cleary would have built a new diocese from the foundations in Nancheng, China; that he would have formed a native clergy of very high quality and distinctive traditions; that as bishop of the diocese with his priests and people he would set very high standards in peace no less than in persecution, which future generations of Nancheng priests and people would find it difficult to emulate.

John Blowick, 'The man of vision', foresaw in 1916 the great missionary revival that was to take place later in the twentieth century. His biographer, I believe, will conclude that Blowick played no small part in bringing that revival about.

Pericles, a famous orator of ancient Greece, claimed that Greek culture, which was brought to faraway places, was woven into the texture of the lives of these faraway peoples. The question must be asked, was the good news of Christianity, which John Blowick and his associates brought to so many countries, was it really woven into the texture of the lives of these far away peoples? In Nancheng diocese, where I was a missionary during the persecution, the good news of Christianity was so inextricably woven into the lives of our people that not even thirty years of savage persecution could extricate it from them.

To illustrate the quality of the Chinese secular priests trained by Bishop Cleary, here is the story of the Kiutu golden bars. But where in the name of heaven would we get golden bars in that remote village in rural China? In the early spring of 1949, just before the Reds came, paper money was worthless. Inflation had ceased to sky-rocket, because the sky was no longer the limit for our inflation. So the bishop was advised to exchange the few thousand American dollars we had for bars of gold. Regardless of which way the situation developed, it was a wise move to have a reserve of hidden gold. If we were all expelled or jailed, the gold would be of great value to our Chinese priests. If, on the other hand, the Reds kept their promise that there would be freedom of religion under their regime, then the gold could be used by the Chinese priests and ourselves.

I knew absolutely nothing about the bishop's plan, until somebody from the orphanage came running excitedly into the priests' house in Kiutu about 5.00 p.m. of an evening in spring and said to me, 'There are three priests coming in the *ma lu* (that was the bridle path which was about a mile from the house) on three bicycles to visit us.' I was always delighted to have visitors, but they rarely came without giving notice. Well, the visitors turned out to be two Chinese priests, Luke Teng and Phil Chou. The third was a Columban, Vincent McNally. They gave me a letter from the bishop and I read it while they went to their rooms to have a wash.

The letter informed me that each of the three priests had brought bars of gold hidden in the hollows of the crossbars in each bike. The idea was that they were to bury that gold in Kiutu, because the bishop and the priests in Nancheng believed that Kiutu was the safest place to bury our treasure. They also felt that if and when the Reds came, Kiutu would be the last place that would get into trouble. All the same, as was his wont, the bishop made allowances for other possibilities. The burial of our treasure, the place it would be buried, was to be kept a secret from me, in case word got out about the gold and that the Communists might torture me in an effort to find out its location.

Anyhow we did our best to get a good meal for them because never before had we visitors who brought us golden bars. After the meal we sat down to have a chat. But the chat never got off the ground. They were preoccupied, wondering and waiting, to figure out what was the most opportune time, and what was the best place to bury the gold – unobserved by any of the local people.

Eventually they went out as darkness was falling, and I kept custody of the eyes while the burial was taking place, but instinctively I knew roughly where the spot was. In about fifteen minutes they were back. Again I tried to launch a conversation, and again failed miserably to get it off the ground. They were tense and worried. Phil Chou, a big stout man who worked on his own little bit of land and had the hands of a farmer, was particularly nervy. His big farmer's hands he was rubbing together and pulling his fingers nervously. Like fidgety Frank in the nursery rhyme, he could not sit still. Vincent McNally, a tall man, well over six feet, was pulling at his pipe at a rate which must have exceeded some speed limit or other. Luke Teng, smaller than Phil Chou but pudgy, was chain smoking, in a hurry. They were obviously worried about the burial place of their treasure. I felt tempted to quote a text from St Luke's gospel: 'For where your treasure is, there will your heart be also.' I decided, however, not to inject any levity into what for them was a serious situation. I probably left the room at this stage, feeling they wanted a private discussion between themselves.

About half an hour later, they told me they did not feel happy about the buried treasure, and that they would go out and try to get a better place. When they returned later I knew instinctively that they had buried the gold at the back of the house. They were more relaxed on their return after the second burial. I felt that there was a sense of job satisfaction and fulfilment about them, which one did not detect after burial number one. Their hearts were no longer where their treasure was, and we had a very enjoyable conversation for a few hours.

The Communists did not agree with the bishop and the priests in Nancheng when they felt that I would be the last to get into trouble. It was as if they said to themselves, 'The last shall be first.' I was the first to get into trouble and I stayed in trouble until it became a way of life for me. With the daily problems and tensions, we forgot about our treasure. The gold brought us no problems while we were in China.

Then, twelve years later, the bishop and I were both based in St Columban's, Dalgan Park, Navan. One evening in September 1965, I went to visit him in his room. He had a detailed map of Kiutu in his hands. 'Oh', he said, as he looked at me over the top of his glasses, 'I had a water diviner here with me and I asked him if he could tell me where our gold is buried in Kiutu – the exact spot.' He then pointed to a spot behind the house and said to me. 'The gold is there.' And indeed that roughly was my understanding of where the second interment had taken place. I am not sure of the value of our buried treasure, but I think it would have been a few thousand American dollars. Then we forgot all about our buried treasure, except on the odd occasion, when I was asked, 'Would you like to go back to China again, if the Communists allowed missionaries into that country?' My stock reply was, 'I would go back in the morning, provided I was given my own parish, Kiutu, including the gold buried within the boundaries of that parish.' The next thing we heard about the gold was when Jim Yang wrote to us. It went as follows: 'Secondly, you will remember the golden bars, left for the future use of the diocese, which we buried in Kiutu. According to the people there, the bars were accidently discovered by some of the pupils of the school built by the Communists. All the gold bars were dug up. So the legacy left by the Columban Fathers is now completely lost. This again reminds us of the truth that man proposes, but God disposes.'

Yes, the legacy we left the Nancheng Catholics in golden bars is now lost, but not the more precious legacy of golden priests whom, under God, we bequeathed to them. All of which brings to mind some lines from Aodh de Blacam's play *Golden Priest*, about St Oliver Plunkett, bishop and martyr, who was martyred in Tyburn over three hundred years ago. The lines are:

> Wooden chalice, golden priest
> When Patrick came to Erin.
> Golden chalice, wooden priest
> And ill the faith was faring.

In the play, Dr Plunkett, then a professor of theology in Rome, says that when he was saying Mass in a Roman church, under a ceiling painted by Michelangelo, he thought of the priests in Ireland, saying Mass at little wayside altars under a sheiling of boughs torn from the trees. And the people were kneeling on the muddy roadway on sops of straw. 'Ah', he exclaims, 'it is they that are the golden priests. We have a verse in the Gaelic', and

BACK TO OUR ROOTS

Dr Plunkett quotes the above lines in English. Some say he composed them himself. His picture of persecution in the Ireland of his day has a lot in common with the persecution in China, in our day.

Golden priests do more to strengthen the faith and to keep it a living and vibrant faith than all the golden bars in Fort Knox.

Epilogue

When I had recovered my health after China, I volunteered to go, as a missionary, to Korea. Our Superior General, Father Tim Connolly, however, had different ideas, and he said 'It is God's will for you to go to London to make our work known there.' I have always been very bad at losing things, but after six months or so in London, my sleep went missing. I am not claiming now to have been a card-holding insomniac, but I have been a very committed fellow traveller, since then. I often thought, as I lay awake at night, of Pascal's words, 'Our Lord is in agony to the end of the world. We must not sleep during that time.' As I tossed and turned, I could not sleep, but I could watch. Some people when they are unable to sleep are very good at praying, but all I could do was watch in darkness and desolation and offer it for the suffering Catholics. In those days, people and priests wanted to hear about China, because it was in the news. While preaching, and speaking, I churned up traumatic experiences which had anything but a tranquilising effect on me when I tried to sleep. Sunday after Sunday, and during the week, I was asked to give talks on China. Be that as it may, I hope that the persecution story will help you to realise that Our Lord is inviting us all to watch with him, to make reparation.

I understand quite a few parish churches throughout the country have Perpetual Adoration. Many of the laity are responding to Our Lord's invitation, 'Could you not watch one hour with me?' Some churches, on the other hand, have adoration before the Blessed Sacrament, just during the day and maybe up to nine or ten at night. St Mary's, Navan, not far from our headquarters here, has Perpetual Adoration. A lady, who is far from young, told me last year that she watched in the early hours of the morning, from two to three, when it was her turn. And she loved it. In Bellevue, near our American headquarters in Omaha, the pastor started Perpetual Adoration in the fifties and it still continues. The generosity and fervour with which our people, in different countries, are participating in this devotion, is the most hopeful sign of the times I have noted.

On the other hand, I think I should say something about the blessings which persecution brings to individuals and to communities. When Jim Yang and John McCormack suffered for their faith, they seemed to grow as Christians, to grow in holiness. But you may say they were only two people, and you have a point in your remark. However, I had the privilege of seeing the blessings of persecution on a community. The community was the parish where I served as pastor when the persecution started, Kiutu. I was expelled during land division, when sufferings and sorrow were the lifestyle of the people whom I served. After I was expelled, I was interned in a military compound in Nancheng, and the Catholics from Kiutu, because they were so poor, were allowed to run the gauntlet and come in to me for Confession and Holy Communion. They also came in, walked the ten miles into Nancheng, for the big feasts. Soon I could notice the difference that persecution made on my people, but I find it very hard to describe that difference. Persecution can bring out the best in us.

In this connection, I often think of some words of Oscar Wilde in his book *De Profundis*. The words are, 'Where there is sorrow, there is holy ground.' Apart from the sorrows and suffering that came to them from the cruelty of the Communists and from their policy of trying to get families to gang up against parents, their most bitter sorrow was when the priest was expelled. Being deprived of the Mass, the Bread of life, for which they hungered, the companionship of the Real Presence – these were their great sorrows. I could see that they suffered a severe pain of loss, but then as they began to come into Nancheng, feast after feast, I began to notice the change. Sorrow seemed to have transformed them as individuals and as a community. Sorrow somehow refines, ennobles, enlightens. Indeed, as I have noted elsewhere, there is a Chinese saying, which goes 'Without sorrow none would become Buddhas' (Buddha means 'enlightened one').

Enlightened by sorrow, the parishioners seemed to have acquired a deeper faith in God and a keener compassion, sympathy and understanding of their fellow men. It was my privilege to witness this beautiful transfiguration on the face of the community I had served, and to realise that somehow in every transfiguration there is something of the Divine. The experience filled me with hope that Providence was at work even then, building Christian cells of resistance, like Kiutu and Nancheng, up and down China, from Harbin to Hong Kong. As far back as 1953, I had the feeling that under God such cells would become strong bastions of Christianity, holding together the threads of their Catholic heritage, till the storms of persecution would have subsided.